Epes Sargent

The Woman who Dared

Epes Sargent

The Woman who Dared

ISBN/EAN: 9783744661300

Printed in Europe, USA, Canada, Australia, Japan

Cover: Foto ©Thomas Meinert / pixelio.de

More available books at **www.hansebooks.com**

THE
WOMAN WHO DARED.

BY

EPES SARGENT.

"Honest liberty is the greatest foe to dishonest license."
JOHN MILTON.

BOSTON:
ROBERTS BROTHERS.
1870.

Entered according to Act of Congress, in the year 1869, by
EPES SARGENT,
in the Clerk's Office of the District Court of the District of Massachusetts.

UNIVERSITY PRESS: WELCH, BIGELOW, & CO.,
CAMBRIDGE.

To —— ——.

SPRING saw my little venture just begun;
    And then your hospitable message came,
Inviting me to taste the strawberries
At Strawberry Hill. I went. How long I stayed,
Urged by dear friends and the restoring breeze,
Let me not say; long enough to complete
My rhythmic structure; day by day it grew,
And all sweet influences helped its growth.
The lawn sloped green and ample till the trees
Met on its margin; and the Hudson's tide
Rolled beautiful beyond, where purple gleams
Fell on the Palisades or touched the hills
Of the opposing shore; for all without
Was but an emblem of the symmetry
I found within, where love held perfect sway,
With taste and beauty and domestic peace
For its allies.
            We do not praise the rose,
Since all who see it know it is the rose;
And so, dear lady, praise of thee would seem,

Dedication.

To all who know thee, quite superfluous.
But if from any of these thoughts be shed
Aught of the fragrance and the hue of truth,
To thee I dedicate the transient flower
In which the eternal beauty reappears;
Knowing, should poison mingle with the sweet,
Thou, like the eclectic bee, with instinct sure,
Wilt take the good alone, and leave the bad.

E. S.

CONTENTS.

		PAGE
I.	OVERTURE	1
II.	THE FATHER'S STORY	7
III.	THE MOTHER'S STORY	39
	Linda's Lullaby	41
IV.	PARADISE FOUND	93
	The Mother's Hymn	100
V.	LINDA	115
	Help me, dear Chords	143
	Be of good Cheer	147
VI.	BY THE SEASIDE	177
	Linda's Song	189
	Under the Pines	203
VII.	FROM LINDA'S DIARY	211
VIII.	FROM MEREDITH'S DIARY	235
IX.	BESIDE THE LAKE	249
NOTES		263

THE WOMAN WHO DARED.

I.

OVERTURE.

Blest Power that canst transfigure common things,
And, like the sun, make the clod burst in bloom, —
Unseal the fount so mute this many a day,
And help me sing of Linda! Why of her,
Since she would shrink with manifest recoil,
Knew she that deeds of hers were made a theme

The Woman who Dared.

For measured verse? Why leave the garden
    flowers
To fix the eye on one poor violet
That on the solitary grove sheds fragrance?
Themes are enough, that court a wide regard,
And prompt a strenuous flight; and yet from all,
My thoughts come back to Linda. Let me spare,
As best I may, her modest privacy,
While under Fancy's not inapt disguise
I give substantial truth, and deal with no
Unreal beings or fantastic facts:
Bear witness to it, Linda!

                      Now while May
Keeps me a restive prisoner in the house,
For the first time the Spring's unkindness ever
Held me aloof from her companionship,
However roughly from the east her breath
Came as if all the icebergs of Grand Bank
Were giving up their forms in that one gust, —

Now while on orchard-trees the struggling blos-
    soms
Break from the varnished cerements, and in clouds
Of pink and white float round the boughs that hold
Their verdure yet in check, — and while the lawn
Lures from yon hemlock hedge the robin, plump
And copper-breasted, and the west wind brings
Mildness and balm, — let me attempt the task
That also is a pastime.

                    What though Spring
Brings not of Youth the wonder and the zest;
The hopes, the day-dreams, and the exultations?
The animal life whose overflow and waste
Would far out-measure now our little hoard?
The health that made mere physical existence
An ample joy; that on the ocean beach
Shared with the leaping waves their breezy glee;
That in deep woods, or in forsaken clearings,
Where the charred logs were hid by verdure new,

And the shy wood-thrush lighted ; or on hills
Whence counties lay outspread beneath our gaze ;
Or by some rock-girt lake where sandy margins
Sloped to the mirrored tints of waving trees, —
Could feel no burden in the grasshopper,
And no unrest in the long summer day?
Would I esteem Youth's fervors fair return
For temperate airs that fan sublimer heights
Than Youth could scale ; heights whence the patient vision
May see this life's harsh inequalities,
Its rudimental good and full-blown evil,
Its crimes and earthquakes and insanities,
And all the wrongs and sorrows that perplex us,
Assume, beneath the eternal calm, the order
Which can come only from a Love Divine ?
A love that sees the good beyond the evil,
The serial life beyond the eclipsing death, —

That tracks the spirit through eternities,
Backward and forward, and in every germ
Beholds its past, its present, and its future,
At every stage beholds it gravitate
Where it belongs, and thence new-born emerge
Into new life and opportunity,
An outcast never from the assiduous Mercy,
Providing for His teeming universe,
Divinely perfect not because complete,
But because incomplete, advancing ever
Beneath the care Supreme? — heights whence
 the soul,
Uplifted from all speculative fog,
All darkening doctrine, all confusing fear,
Can see the drifted plants, can scent the odors,
That surely come from that celestial shore
To which we tend; however out of reckoning,
Swept wrong by Error's currents, Passion's
 storms,
The poor tossed bark may be?

Descend, my thoughts!
Your theme lies lowly as the ground-bird's nest;
Why seek, with wings so feeble and unused,
To soar above the clouds and front the stars?
Descend from your high venture, and to scenes
Of the heart's common history come down!

II.

THE FATHER'S STORY.

THE little mansion had its fill of sunshine;
　　The western windows overlooked the Hudson
Where the great city's traffic vexed the tide;
The front received the Orient's early flush.
Here dwelt three beings, who the neighbors said
Were husband, wife, and daughter; and indeed
There was no sign that they were otherwise.
Their name was Percival; they lived secluded,
Saw no society, except some poor

Old pensioner who came for food or help;
Though, when fair days invited, they would take
The omnibus and go to see the paintings
At the Academy; or hear the music
At opera or concert; then, in summer,
A visit to the seaside or the hills
Would oft entice them.

      Percival had reached
His threescore years and five, but stood erect
As if no touch of age had chilled him yet.
Simple in habit, studious how to live
In best conformity with laws divine, —
Impulsive, yet by trial taught to question
All impulses, affections, appetites,
At Reason's bar, — two objects paramount
Seemed steadily before him; one, to find
The eternal truth, showing the constant right
In politics, in social life, in morals, —
The other, to apply all love and wisdom
To education of his child — of Linda.

The Father's Story.

Yet, if with eye anointed, you could look
On that benign and tranquil countenance,
You might detect the lines which Passion leaves
Long after its volcano is extinct
And flowers conceal its lava. Percival
Was older than his consort, twenty years;
Yet were they fitly mated; though, with her,
Time had dealt very gently, leaving face
And rounded form still youthful, and unmarred
By one uncomely outline; hardly mingling
A thread of silver in her chestnut hair
That affluent needed no deceiving braid.
Framed for maternity the matron seemed:
Thrice had she been a mother; but the children,
The first six winters of her union brought,
A boy and girl, were lost to her at once
By a wall's falling on them, as they went,
Heedless of danger, hand in hand, to school.
To either parent terrible the blow!
But, three years afterward, when Linda came,

With her dark azure eyes and golden hair,
It was as if a healing angel touched
The parents' wound, and turned their desolation
Into a present paradise, revealing
Two dear ones, beckoning from the spirit-land,
And one, detaining them, with infant grasp,
Feeble, yet how resistless! here below.

And so there was great comfort in that household:
And those unwhispered longings both had felt
At times, that they might pass to other scenes
Where Love would find its own, were felt no more:
For Linda grew in beauty every day;
Beauty not only of the outward mould,
Sparkling in those dear eyes, and on the wind
Tossing those locks of gold, but beauty born,
In revelations flitting o'er the face,
From the soul's inner symmetry; from love

Too deep and pure to utter, had she words;
From the divine desire to know; to prove
All objects brought within her dawning ken;
From frolic mirth, not heedless but most apt;
From sense of conscience, shown in little things
So early; and from infant courtesy
Charming and debonair.
      The parents said,
While the glad tears shone brimming in their eyes,
"Oh! lacking love and best experience
Are those who tell us that the purity
And innocence of childhood are delusion;
Or that, so far as they exist, they show
The absence of all mind; no impulses
Save those of selfish passion moving it!
And that, by nature desperately wicked,[1]
The child learns good through evil; having no
Innate ideas, no inborn will, no bias.
Here, in this infant, is our confutation!

O self-sufficing physiologist,
Who, grubbing in the earth, hast missed the stars,
We ask no other answer to thy creed
Than this, the answer heaven and earth supply

Now sixteen summers had our Linda seen,
And grown to be a fair-haired, winsome maid,
In shape and aspect promising to be
A softened repetition of her mother;
And yet some traits from the paternal side
Gave to the head an intellectual grace
And to the liquid eyes a power reserved,
Brooding awhile in tender gloom, and then
Flashing emotion, as some lofty thought,
Some sight of pity, or some generous deed,
Kindled a ready sympathy whose tears
Fell on no barren purpose; for with Linda
To feel, to be uplifted, was to act;
Her sorest trials being when she found
How far the wish to do outran the power.

The Father's Story.

Often would Percival observe his child,
And study to divine if in the future
Of that organization, when mature,
There should prevail the elements that lead
Woman to find the crowning charm of life
In the affections of a happy marriage,
Or if with satisfactions of the mind
And the æsthetic faculty, the aims
Of art and letters, the pursuits of trade,
Linda might find the fresh activities
He craved for her, and which forecasting care
Might possibly provide.
                          His means were small,
Merged in a life-annuity which gave
All that he held as indispensable
To sanative conditions in a home:
Good air, good influences, proper food.
By making his old wardrobe do long service
He saved the wherewith to get faithful help
From the best teachers in instructing Linda;

And she was still the object uppermost.
Dawned the day fair, for Linda it was fair,
And they all three could ramble in the Park.
If on Broadway the ripe fruit tempted him,
Linda was fond of fruit; those grapes will do
For Linda. Was the music rich and rare?
Linda must hear it. Were the paintings grand?
Linda must see them. So the important thought
Was always Linda; and the mother shared
In all this fond parental providence;
For in her tender pride in the dear girl
There was no room for any selfish thought,
For any jealous balancing of dues.

"My child," said Percival, one summer day,
As he brought in a bunch of snow-white roses,
Ringed with carnations, many-leafed and fragrant,
"Take it, an offering for your birthday; this
Is June the twelfth, a happy day for me."
"How fresh, how beautiful!" said Linda rising

And kissing him on either cheek. "Dear
    father,
You spoil me for all other care, I fear,
Since none can be like yours."
                      "Why speak of that?"
He with a start exclaimed; "my care must be
Prolonged till I can see you safely fixed
In an assured and happy womanhood.
Why should it not be so? Though sixty-five,
How well am I, and strong! No, Linda, no;
Dream not of other tendance yet awhile;
My father lived to eighty, and his father
To eighty-five; and I am stronger now
Than they were, at my age."
                      "Live long!" cried Linda,
"For whom have I to love me, to befriend,
You and my mother gone?"
                      "Your mother, child?
She should outlive me by some twenty years
At least. God grant, her sweet companionship

May be your strength and light when I 'm not
    here,
My matchless little girl, my precious Linda!"

"Ah! how Love magnifies the thing it loves!"
Smiling she said: "when I look in the glass,
I see a comely Miss; nay, perhaps pretty;
That epithet is her superlative,
So far as person is concerned, I fear.
Grant her a cheerful temper; that she gets
From both her parents. She is dutiful, —
No wonder, for she never is opposed!
Strangely coincident her way is yours;
Industrious, but that 's her mother's training.
Then if you come to gifts of mind — ah me!
What can she show? We 'll not pronounce her
    dull;
But she 's not apt or quick; and all she gets
Is by hard work, by oft-repeated trials,
Trials with intermissions of despair.

The languages she takes to not unkindly ;
But mathematics is her scourge, her kill-joy,
Pressing her like a nightmare. Logic, too,
Distresses and confuses her poor brain ;
Oh! ask her not for reasons. As for music —
Music she loves. Would that Love might inspire
The genius it reveres so ardently!
Has she no gift for painting? Eye for form
And coloring I truly think she has ;
And one thing she can do, and do it well ;
She can group flowers and ferns and autumn
      leaves,
Paint their true tints, and render back to nature
A not unfaithful copy.
                "This the extent
Of her achievements! She has labored hard
To mould a bust or statue ; but the clay
Lacked the Pygmalion touch beneath her hands.
She 'll never be a female Angelo.
She must come down content to mother Earth,

And study out the alphabet which Summer
Weaves on the sod in fields or bordering woods.
Such is your paragon, my simple father!
But now, this ordinary little girl,
So seeming frank, (whisper it low!) is yet
So deep, so crafty, and so full of wiles,
That she has quite persuaded both her parents —
In most things sensible, clear-seeing people —
That she is just a prodigy indeed!
Not one of goodness merely, but of wit,
Capacity, and general cleverness!"

"There, that will do, spoilt darling! What a
        tongue!"
Percival said, admiring while he chided.
"O the swift time! Thou 'rt seventeen to-day;
And yet, except thy parents and thy teachers,
Friends and companions thou hast hardly known.
'T is fit that I should tell thee why our life
Has been thus socially estranged and quiet.

The Father's Story.

Sit down, and let me push the arm-chair up
Where I can note the changes in thy face;
For 't is a traitor, that sweet face of thine,
And has a sign for every fleeting thought.

"But here 's our little mother! Come, my dear,
And take a seat by Linda; thou didst help me
To graft upon the bitter past a fruit
All sweetness, and thy very presence now
Can take the sting from a too sad remembrance."

The mother placed her hand upon his brow
And said: "The water-lily springs from mud;
So springs the future from the past." Then he:
"My father's death made me, at twenty-one,
Heir to a fortune which in those slow days
Was thought sufficient: I had quitted Yale
With some slight reputation as a scholar,
And, in the first flush of ingenuous youth
When brave imagination's rosy hue

Tinges all unknown objects, I was launched
Into society in this great place; —
Sisterless, motherless, and having seen
But little, in my student life, of women.

"All matrons who had marriageable girls
Looked on me as their proper prey, and spread
Their nets to catch me; and, poor, verdant youth,
Soon I was caught, — caught in a snare indeed,
Though by no mother's clever management.
Young, beautiful, accomplished, she, my Fate,
Met me with smiles, and doomed me while she smiled
Nimble as light, fluent as molten lead
To take the offered mould, — apt to affect
Each preference of taste or sentiment
That best might flatter, — affable and kind,
Or seeming so, — and generous to a fault, —
But that was when she had a part to play, —
Affectionate — ah! there too she was feigning —

The Father's Story.

As I look calmly back, to me she seems
The simple incarnation of a mind
Possessed of all the secrets of the heart,
And quick to substitute a counterfeit
For the heart's genuine coin, and make it pass;
But void of feeling as the knife that wounds!
And so the game was in her hands, and she
Played it with confident, remorseless skill
Even to the bitter end.

      " Yet do not think
The inner prescience never stirred or spoke:
Veiled though it be from consciousness so
  strangely,
And its fine voice unheard amid the din
Of outward things, the quest of earthly passion,
There is an under-sense, a faculty
All independent of our mortal organs,
And circumscribed by neither space nor time.
Else whence proceed they, those clairvoyant
  glimpses,

That vision piercing to the distant future,
Those quick monitions of impending ruin,
If not from depths of soul which consciousness,
Limited as it is in mortal scope,
May not explore? Yet there serenely latent,
Or with a conscious being all their own,
Superior and apart from what we know
In this close keep we call our waking state,
Lie growing with our growth the lofty powers
We reck not of; which some may live a life
And never heed, nor know they have a soul;
Which many a plodding anthropologist,
Philosopher, logician, scientist,
Ignore as moonshine; but which are, no less,
Actual, proven, and, in their dignity
And grasp and space-defying attributes,
Worthy to qualify a deathless spirit
To have the range of an infinity
Through an unending period — at once
A promise and a proof of life immortal.

The Father's Story.

"One night, one mild, sweet night in early June,
We two had paced the drawing-room together
Till ten o'clock, and then I took my leave
And walked along the street, a square or more,
When suddenly I looked up at a star,
And then, a thought I could not fail to heed,
From the soul's awful region unexplored,
Rushed, crying, 'Back! Go back!' And back
    I went,
As hastily as if it were a thing
Of life or death. I did not stop to pull
The door-bell, but sprang up alert and still
To the piazza of the open window,
Drew back a blind inaudibly, looked in,
And through the waving muslin curtain, saw —
Well, she was seated in a young man's lap,
Her head upon his shoulder.

                    "Quick of ear
As the chased hare, she heard me; started up,
Ran to the curtain, eagerly drew me in,

And said, while joy beamed tender in her eyes,
'My brother Ambrose, just arrived from Europe!'
So swift she was, she did not give me time
Even for one jealous pang. I took his hand,
And saying, 'Anna's brother must be mine,'
I bade them both good-night, and went my way:
So was I fooled, — my better angel baffled!

"And yet once more the vivid warning came,
Flashed like quick truth from her own eyes. We
  stood
Together in a ball-room, when a lady,
To me unknown, came up, regarded me
With strange compassion in her curious glance,
And then, with something less divine than pity,
Looked down on my betrothed, and moved away.
I turned to Anna, but upon her face,
There was a look to startle like a ghost;
Defiance, deadly fear, and murderous hate
Were all so wildly blended! But 't was gone —

Gone like a flash before I well could mark it;
And in its place there came a luminous smile,
So childlike sweet, such type of heavenly candor,
It would have served for a Madonna's mouth,
To make the pilgrim's adoration easy.
'Who was that lady, Anna?' I inquired.
'A Mrs. Lothian,' was her reply:
'A lovely person, although somewhat haughty.'
We returned home soon after, and no more
Was said of it.

    " The rapid weeks flew by,
And Anna plied her powers to charm, but still
Not all the subtle glamour of her presence
Could bind in sleep my pleading monitor.
And so at last I said : 'We both are young:
Let us, as earnest of a mutual wish
To share a perfect love, or none at all,
Absolve each other here, without condition,
From this engagement ; and, if three years hence
We both are of one heart, then shall we find

The means to make it known; of that be sure!
Are you in your own loyalty so fixed
As to accept the challenge? Would you prize
The love of any man, who could not bear
A test so simple?'

"The first word I spoke
Made all my meaning plain to her; she shook,
But more perhaps with anger than with grief;
She turned her face away, and covered it
With both her hands, and so remained until
I had done speaking; then she rose at once,
Her face averted still, (she durst not show it!)
And grasped my hand, and, in a husky tone
Sheathing her wrath, exclaimed: 'To-morrow, come
At twelve — at twelve!' and rushed out of the room.

"Prompt at the hour I went; and in the parlor
Sat down expectant; and she entered soon,

Clad all in white; upon her face the marks
Of passionate tears, and a beseeching sorrow
In every look! A desk of ivory,
Borne in her hands, she placed upon the table;
I rose to meet her, but she motioned me
To keep my seat; then, with an arm thrown over
A high-backed chair, as if to keep from falling,
(The attitude was charming, and she knew it),
She said: 'Take back the little desk you gave me;
In it are all your letters, — all your gifts.
Take them, and give me mine.'
"The last few words
Came as if struggling through a crowd of sobs.
What could I do but lead her to the sofa,
Sit by her side, take her white hand, and say:
'This is no final separation, Anna;
It is a trial merely of our loves?'

"'A light affair perhaps to you,' she said,
'But death to me. As whim or pleasure points,

You can go here, go there, and lead the life
You most affect ; while I, the home-kept slave
Of others' humors, must brave poverty,
Neglect and cruel treatment.' — ' Did you say
Poverty, Anna ? ' — ' Do not breathe a word
Of what I tell you : father is a bankrupt,
Or soon will be ; and we shall be compelled
To quit our freestone house, and breathe the air
Of squalid want.   From that I 'd not recoil,
Could I have loving looks and words ; for what
Is poverty if there 's but love to gild it ?
Ah ! poverty ' — ' Nay, Anna, poverty
You shall not know, only accept from me
The means to fix you in becoming plenty.'
' Never ! ' she cried ; ' ah ! cruel to propose it ! '
And then more tears ; till, touched and foiled, I
      said,
Looking her in the face while she gazed up
In mine with eager tenderness, — ' Accept
A happy home, if I can help to make it.
We will be married, Anna, when you please.'

The Father's Story.

"And so she had her way, and we were married;
And the next day all Wall Street was aroused
By news that brave Papa had won renown
Not simply as a bankrupt, but a swindler,
Escaping, by the skin of his teeth, the Tombs.
'No matter! Papa has a son-in-law,
A greenhorn, as they say, who occupies
A stately house on the Fifth Avenue,
And, in his hall, Papa will hang his hat.'
And, in all this, Rumor but hit the truth.

"Six months rolled by. Repeatedly I asked,
'Where's Brother Ambrose?' He, it seems, was held
In such request by government, that rarely
Could he be spared for home enjoyment; but
At length I did encounter Brother Ambrose,
And once again I found him —

     "Well, the scales
Dropped from my eyes. I asked no other proof

Than a quick look I saw the two exchange, —
Forgetful of a mirror at their side, —
To see I was betrayed. He was no brother.
I sought more proof; but they, imagining
I knew more than I did, were swift to act.
Before I could find steps for a divorce
She stole a march upon me, and herself
Took the initiative, and played the victim,
Nipping me as a culprit in the law.

"It was a plot so dexterously framed,
All the precautions and contrivances
Were with such craft foreplanned; the perjuries
Were all so well adjusted; my pure life
Was made to seem so black; the witnesses
Were so well drilled, so perfect in their parts, —
In short, it was a work of art so thorough,
I did not marvel at the Court's decision,
Which was, for her, — divorce and alimony;
For me, — no freedom, since no privilege
Of marrying again. Such the decree!"

"I'm glad you spurned it as you did!" cried
    Linda,
While her cheeks flushed, and hot, indignant tears,
Responded to her anger.   Then she kissed
Her father on each cheek, and tenderly
Embraced her mother too ; and they, the while,
With a slight moisture in their smiling eyes,
Exchanged a nod.   Then Percival to Linda:
" Why, what an utter rebel you would be,
You little champion of the higher law !
Sit down, and hear me out."
                      " If such their justice,"
Cried Linda, irrepressible and panting,
" Who would not spurn it, and hurl back defiance
To all the Justice Shallows on the Bench —
To them and their decrees ! "
                      " My little girl,"
The father said, " the heart's impulsive choice
May guide us safely when the act must be
Born of the instant, but let Reason rule

When Reason may.) For some twelve years, I lived
A wandering life in Europe ; not so crushed
By my most harsh experience but I
Could find, in study and in change of scene,
How much of relish life has for the mind
As well as the affections ; still I felt
Mine was a nature in which these must play
No secondary part ; and so the void
Enlarged as age drew nearer ; and at forty
A weariness of life came over me,
And I was sick at heart ; for many a joy
Had lost the charm that made it joy. I took
A house in London, all for solitude,
And there got what you may not find in Egypt,
Or on Mont Blanc.

    " One day as I was crossing
An obscure street, I saw a crowd of workmen
Gathered around a man upon the ground :
A rafter from a half-built house had fallen,

And he was badly injured. Seeing none
To act with promptness in the case, I hailed
A cab, and had him driven to my house.
Finding he was a fellow-countryman,
I gave him one of my spare rooms, and sent
For the best surgeon near. His report was,
The wound itself was nothing serious,
But there was over-action of the brain,
Quite independent, which might lead to danger,
Unless reduced in season ; and the patient
Should have the best of watching and attendance,
And not be left to brood on any trouble,
But be kept cheerful. Then with some directions
For diet, sedatives, and laxatives,
The doctor bowed, received his fee, and left.
My guest lay sad and silent for a while,
Then turned to me and said: 'My name is Ken-
  rick ;
I'm from Chicago — was a broker there.
A month ago my wife eloped from me ;·

And her companion, as you may surmise,
Was one I had befriended — raised from nothing.
I'm here upon their track."

"'Why so?' I asked.
'What do you want of them?' — 'What do I
    want?'
He stretched his eyes at me inquiringly.
'How strange,' said I, 'the inconsistency!
Here's a true man would try to overtake
An untrue mate! If she's not sterling gold
And loyal as the loadstone, — not alone
In every act, but every thought and throb, —
Why should you care who puts her to the proof,
Takes her away, and leaves you free again?
Show me 't is an illusion I adore,
And I will thank you, though it be in anguish.
To no false gods I bow, if I can help it!'

"'Could I,' said Kenrick, 'have him only once
Where I could take him by the throat, and meas-
    ure

My strength with his!'—'Tut, tut! the kind
    physician
Who warns you of some lurking taint, to which
The cautery should be applied at once,
Is not, in act, if not intent, your friend
More certainly than he you rave against.
And you 've been jealous, I suppose, at times,
Of the poor runaway?'—'Ay, that I have!
Bitterly jealous.'
        "'Jealousy and love
Were never yet true mates; for jealousy
Is born of selfish passion, lust, or pride,
While love is so divine and pure a thing,
It only takes what cannot be withheld.
It flies constraint. All that it gives is given,
Even as the lily renders up its perfume,
Because it cannot help it. Would it crave
Return less worthy? Would it be content
With a grudged gift? Then it is something else,
Not love — not love! Ah me! how men and
    women

Cozen themselves with words, and let their pas-
    sions
Fool them and blind, until they madly hug
Illusions which some stunning shock like yours
Puts to the proof, revealing emptiness.
Have you a loving heart, and would you feed it
On what the swine have left, — mock it with
    lies?'
'Speak this to me again, when I am stronger,'
Said Kenrick, smiling faintly. Then I left him,
And taking up 'The Times' looked thro' the list
Of 'Wants'; and one amid the many hundred
Instantly caught my eye. It merely said:
'Wanted, by a young woman, strong and healthy,
A place as nurse for any invalid.
Address 681, Times Office.' So
I wrote and told 681 to call
Upon me at a certain hour.
                              "And now,
My dear, this little girl with eager eyes

Has, for a summer morning, heard enough.
The weather is the crown of all that June
Has of most fair, — the year's transcendent day;
When the young foliage and the perfect air
Intoxicate the birds, and put our hearts
In harmony with their extravagance
Of joy and love. Come, come! To slight this day
Would be a sin. We'll ramble in the Park,
And take our dinner there, and see the flowers,
The children, and the swans, and all the places
Which Linda used to love in babyhood,
When, in her little carriage, like a queen
She'd sit, receiving homage from all eyes."

The father had his way; and in the Park
They spent the happy time, and felt the charm
Which harmony complete with Nature brings
When loving spirits, unpreoccupied,
Gain by surrender, and grow rich by giving.

O sunshine and blue sky and genial airs!
To human happiness, like daily bread,
Your blessings come, till the unthinking heart
Recks not the debt we owe your silent powers.
If ye can give so much, what may not He
Of whose omnipotence ye are but shadows
Have in reserve in his eternities!

III.

THE MOTHER'S STORY.

THAT evening, when the feast of strawberries
  Had been partaken, and the happy three
Sat down together, Linda asked: "And now,
May I not hear the rest?"—"To-morrow, Linda,
You shall hear all," said Percival; "but now,
That brain of yours must tranquillize itself
Before you try to sleep; and so, to-night,
Let us have 'Annie Laurie,' 'Bonnie Doon,'
And songs that most affront the dainty ear
Of modern fashion." Linda played and sang

A full half-hour; then, turning on her chair,
Said, "Now shall mother sing that cradle ditty
You made for me, an infant. Mother, mine,
Imagine you are rocking me to sleep,
As in those far-off days."

                            Replied the mother:
"O the dear days! yet not more dear than
    these!
For frugal Linda brings along with her
All of her past; the infant's purity,
The child's confiding love, and now, at last,
The maiden's free and quick intelligence!
Be ever thus, my Linda; for the pure
In heart shall carry an immortal youth
Into the great to-come. That little song —
Well I remember the delightful time
When 't was extemporized; when, with my pen,
I noted down the words, while, by your crib,
Your father sat, and you, with little fists
Drawn tight, would spring and start, as infants
    will,

Crowing the while, and chuckling at the words
Not comprehended yet, save in the smiles
That with them went! 'T was at the mellow
    close
Of an autumnal day, and we were staying
In a secluded village, where a brook
Babbled beneath our window, and the hum
Of insects soothed us, while a louder note
From the hoarse frog's bassoon would, now and
    then,
Break on the cricket's sleepy monotone
And startle laughter." Here the matron paused;
Then sweeping, with a firm, elastic touch,
The ivory keys, sang

LINDA'S LULLABY.

I.

Murmur low, little rivulet flowing!
For to sleep our dear Linda is going;
All good little lambs be reposing,
For Linda one eyelid is closing.

II.

O frogs! what a noise you are making!
O crickets! now don't keep her waking!
Stop barking, you little dog Rover,
Till Linda can get half-seas over.

III.

Little birds, let our word of love reach you, —
Go to bed, go to sleep, I beseech you;
On her little white coverlet lying,
To sleep our dear Linda is trying.

IV.

Hush! sing just as softly as may be;
Sing lullaby, lullaby, baby!
Now to sleep this dear Linda is going, —
Murmur low, little rivulet flowing!

The next day, when the heat kept all at home,
And they were gathered in the library,
Where fitfully a lazy southern breeze
Would stir the languid curtains, Percival
Said, turning to the mother: "Mary, now
Your story best will supplement my own;

Tell it." She answered: "Let it be so, then;
My life is but the affluent to yours,
In which it found its amplitude and rest.

  My parents dwelt in Liverpool; my father,
A prosperous merchant, gave to business
His time and active thoughts, and let his wife
Rule all beside with rigor absolute.
My maiden name was Mary Merivale.
There were eight daughters of us, and of these
I was the fourth. We lived in liberal style,
And did not lack the best society
The city could afford. My heedful mother,
With eight undowered girls to be disposed of,
Fearfully healthy all, and clamorous
For clothes and rations, entered on a plan
To which she steadily adhered: it was,
To send the younger fry to boarding-schools,
And keep one virgin only, at a time,
And she the oldest, on her hands to marry.

So they came forward in their order: Julia,
And Isabel, and Caroline; until
I was dragged forth from maps and lexicons,
Slate-pencils and arithmetics, and put
Candidate Number Four, upon the list.

"My elder sisters had been all 'well-married';
That is, to parties able to provide
Establishments that Fashion would not scorn;
What more could be desired by loving parents?
As for resistance to her will, when once
She set her heart upon a match, my mother
Would no more bear it than a general
Would bear demur from a subordinate
When ordered into action. If a daughter,
When her chance offered, and was checked as
    good,
Presumed, from any scruple of dislike,
To block the way for her successor, then
Woe to that daughter, and no peace for her

Did she not, with an utter selfishness,
Stand in her younger sister's light? imperil
The poor child's welfare? doom her possibly
To an old maid's forlorn and cheerless lot?

"And so, with an imperious will, my mother
Would sweep away all hindrances, all doubts.
She was, besides, the slave of system; having
Adopted once the plan of bringing forward
No daughter till the previous one was mated,
It was a sacred custom; 't was her own!
It had worked well; must not be broken through.
So my poor sisters went; and some of them
With doubting hearts.

                    "In me, my zealous mother
Found metal not so malleable quite.
One of my teachers at the boarding-school,
A little woman who got scanty pay
For teaching us in French and German, fed
Her lonely heart with dreams of what, some day,

Shall lift her sex to nobler life. She took
A journal called 'The Good Time Coming,'
　　filled
With pleadings for reform of many kinds, —
In education, physical and mental,
Marriage, the rights of women, modes of living.
Weekly I had the reading of it all;
Some of it crude enough, some apt and just,
Forcibly put, and charged with vital facts.
At last these had for me a fascination
That quite eclipsed the novels of the day.

"I learnt, that, bound up in the moral law,
Are laws of health and physical control,
Unheeded in the family and school;
How fashion, stupid pride, and love of show,
The greed of gain, or the pursuit of pleasure,
Empty and frivolous, make men and women
False to their natures, cruel to each other
And to the unborn offspring they devote

To misery through ill-assorted unions,
Or habits reckless of maternal dues;
How marriage, sacredest of mortal steps,
Is entered on from motives all unworthy;
Social ambition, mercenary aims,
The dread of poverty, of singleness, —
The object of uniting families, —
And momentary passion fatuous.
So I resolved, God helping, to be true
To my own self, and that way true to all.

"The fête that signalized my coming out
Was, so my mother said, the costliest yet.
Whole greenhouses were emptied to adorn
Our rooms with flowers; a band played in the hall;
The supper-table flashed with plate and silver
And Dresden ware and bright Bohemian glass;
The wines and viands were profuse and rare;
And everybody said, 't was a grand ball.

"But what of her, for whom it was the flourish
Of trumpets blown to celebrate her entrance
Into society? Let others speak!
These the remarks I had to overhear:
'She's rather pretty.' — 'Pretty is the word.'
'But not so dashing as the elder sisters.'
'Cleverer though, perhaps,' — 'She takes it coolly.
Her heart's not in the ball; that's evident.'
'Where is it? Is she bookish?' — 'So I've
    heard.'
'Unlike the rest, then.' — 'That straw-colored
    silk
Should have had flounces.' — 'Is that hair her
    own?'
'I think so?' — 'She's no dancer.' — 'Apathetic
As any duchess.' — 'The young men seem shy;
She does n't put them at their ease, 't is plain.'
'See, the old woman chides her; she deserves it;
She'll not pick up admirers if she plays
My Lady Cool so grandly. Watch mamma.

The hook is nicely baited; where are all
The gudgeons it should lure?   I marvel not
Mamma is in a fluster ; tap, tap, tap,
See her fan go!   No strategy, no effort,
No dandy-killing shot from languid eyes,
On that girl's part !   And all this fuss for her !'

"The gossips, in these random whisperings,
Made some good shots, that failed not of the
     mark.
The lights, the roses, the voluptuous music,
The shining robes, the jewels, the bright faces
Engrossed me not so much as one pale face,
Youthful but pinched, which I had seen a moment,
An hour before, reflected in the mirror
At which I stood while nimble dressing-maids
Helped to array me.   A poor girl had brought
The bodice of my silken robe, on which
She had been working closely ; and my mother

Chided her for delay ; but no reply
Was made, save only what the pleading eyes
Could not withhold.   Then tendering a scrap
Of paper, record of her paltry charge,
She meekly stood.   'Pooh! bring it here next
    week,'
My mother said.   'No!' turning round, I cried ;
'Let her be paid at once ; there must be money
In the house somewhere ; it may be a loss,
An inconvenience, for her to come back
Just for a trifling sum.' — 'Impertinent!'
My mother kindling, cried.   'Do you rule here?'
'I can return,' timidly said the girl.
Then a gold thimble from my drawer I took,
And offered it, remarking, 'Keep or sell it,
To hold you good for all your wasted time.'
'My time, — what is it worth?' replied the girl,
Motioning her refusal, but with smiles
Of speechless gratitude, and then escaping
Before I could prevent her.

"'Novel-reading
Has brought you to this insipidity,'
My mother said: 'such sentimental pap,
You never got from me. Come, hurry down;
Put off that sullen look. The carriages
Begin to roll; the guests are on the stairs.
Learn to command your smiles, my dear. Now
    go.'

"So down I went, but in no conquering mood.
I did not scrutinize the festive dresses;
Of the sad hearts I thought, the poor thin hands
That put of life somewhat in every stitch
For a grudged pittance. All disguises fell;
Voices betrayed the speakers in their tones,
Despite of flattering words; and smiles revealed
The weariness or hatred they would hide.
And so, preoccupied and grave, I looked
On all the gayety; and reigning belles
Took heart to find in me no coming rival.

"Lent now was near; the time of all diversion
And visiting was over; and my mother
Summed up her griefs in this one lamentation:
'The season gone, and not one offer yet!
You, Mary, are the first one of my daughters
Whose coming-out so flat a failure proved.
Think of your sister Julia; her first winter
Brought Hammersley to her feet. A splendid
    match!
First cousin to a lord! How envious
Were all the dowagers at my success!
If I've not done all that a mother could,
Tell me wherein I've failed. Yet one year more
I shall allow you for your trial. Then,
If you have made no step in the direction
Of matrimony, why, you must go off
To Ireland, to America, or France,
And leave the field for your next younger
For Susan.' — 'She is welcome to it now,'
I said, with something like disdain, I fear,

In my cold smile. — 'My plans are laid, you know,'
Replied my mother; 'find your duty in
A simple acquiescence; I know best.'

"'T is said the woman always is to blame
If a man ventures to commit himself
In a proposal unacceptable.
The rule has its exceptions; for I gave
No word, no inkling of encouragement
To Captain Dudley; yet I had an offer
From Captain Dudley. Young, and elegant,
Though of a stock somewhat attenuate;
Rich, though a younger son; a gentleman,
A scholar, — what good reason could I give
For saying Nay to such an applicant?
'Explain!' my mother cried, with brow severe;
'Is not his character without a flaw?'
'So far as known to me.' — 'Is he a fool?'
'Far from it; culture and good sense are his.'
'Could you not love him?' — 'Very tenderly,

Perhaps, with time to aid.' — 'Has any one
Preoccupied your heart?' — 'My heart is free,
And has been always free.' — 'Indeed? Then why
Refuse to be the wife of this young man?'
'Simply because he's not the man I'd choose
To be the father of a child of mine.'

"If I had put a pistol at her head,
My lady mother would not so have started.
'What! a mere girl — and you can entertain
Such thoughts! so selfish, gross, unmaidenly!'
'If,' I replied, 'I'm old enough to dream
Of marriage, as you bid me, then 't is time
For me to think of all the risk I run.
Selfish, you call it; gross, unmaidenly;
Is it unmaidenly to hesitate
In the surrender of my maiden state?
Your epithets belong to those who fail
To think at all, or only think of this :

What's the man's income? Will he let me have
A house in the right quarter? Keep a carriage?
And is he in society? Such women
Plant nightshade, and affect to wonder why
The growth is not of lilies and carnations!'

"'So! just let loose from school,' replied my
  mother,
'You'd teach me what is womanly! Pert minx!
Tell me in simple English what you mean
By your objections to this match, so largely
Above your merits?'—'This is what I mean:
For reasons that are instincts more than reasons,
And therefore not to be explained to those
Who in them do not share, as you do not,
I would not wed this man,—not if I loved him.'
'Enough! You've had your turn; and now pre-
  pare
To make a visit to your father's cousin
In Nova Scotia; there, perhaps, you may

Find a congenial mate among the clowns
And roughs provincial. Go and pack your trunk.
Fool your own opportunities away ;
You shall not thrust your sister out of hers.'

"I did not pack my trunk ; another suitor,
One twice as rich as Dudley, kindled hopes
Anew in my poor mother's breast ; and so
Susan was kept at school another season,
And I was put upon the course once more,
My training perfect and my harness new !

" Who could object to Arthur Pennington ?
Son of a wealthy manufacturer,
A type he was of English adolescence,
Trained by harmonious culture to the fulness
Of all that Nature had supplied ; a person
That did not lack one manly grace ; a mind
Which took the mould that social pressure gave,
Without one protest native to itself.

In the accepted, the conventional,
He looked for Truth, nor ever had a doubt
Whether she might not hide in some deep well
Rather than flaunt her modest purity
In dusty highways. With my disposition
To challenge all that human dogmatism
Imperious would impose upon my thought,
What pretty yoke-fellows for life should we,
Arthur and I, have been! Misled by hopes
Which were inspired too fondly by my mother,
He, too, proposed, and was of course rejected.

"Then the storm broke! The cup of my offences
Was overflowed at last. Now must I go —
Go, where she cared not; only disappear
From her domain; she washed her hands of me!
Hundreds of pounds had been invested in me, —
My dresses, jewelry, and entertainments, —
And here was the result! But no more money,
From her, must I expect; my father's income

Had not for years been equal to his outlays.
Any day he might be compelled to change
His style of living ; all had been kept up
For the advantage of myself and sisters ;
And here was all the gratitude I showed !

"This time my mother was in earnest ; so
Now must I lay my plans to go at once.
Whither ? to seek a transient home with one
Of my own married sisters ? Ah ! the thought
Of being dependent galled me like a spur.
No ! go to work, — a voice within me said :
Think of the many thousands of your sex
Who, young and giddy, not equipped like you,
Are thrown upon the world to battle with it
As best they may ! Now try your closet virtue ;
See if your theory can stand the proof, —
If trial will not warp your sense of right.
When Poverty shall dog your every step,
And at your scanty or unwholesome meal

The Mother's Story.   59

Sit down, or with you, in your thin attire,
Go shivering home at night from ill-paid toil, —
Then see if you can keep your feet from straying;
Then choose as only Conscience bids you choose!

"The sewing-girl who worked upon my dress,
The day of the great ball, was Lucy Merle;
I found her saving up her petty means
To go to London, to get better wages, —
And said: 'Well, Lucy, let us go together.'
She sold some jewels for me, and we went.

"In London! two unfriended girls in London!
We hired a room, and got employment soon,
Such as it was; but small the recompense!
Though Lucy, quicker at her work than I,
Could earn enough to live upon — almost.
For her the change was slight.
      "A year we toiled
In company; and I 'll not tell you all

The hardships, trials, wrongs, we underwent.
In my blue trunk you 'll find a little pistol,
Got for our joint protection in those days.
May it be near you, should you ever need it!
Finding, at length, I could no longer earn
My share of our expenses by the needle,
I sought a situation as a nurse.
And in 'The Times' I advertised my 'Want.'
An answer came, directing me to call
Upon the writer at a certain hour.
I went. I met a man of middle age
Whose name was Percival. I thought his manner
Was coldly kind.

     " 'You 're very young,' he said,
'To fill the situation of a nurse.
What reference have you?' Not a distant
   thought
Of such a need had ever troubled me!
'I bring,' said I, 'no reference.' — 'That 's a pity.
What pledge have I of character?' — 'Not any.'

The Mother's Story.

And then, impatient at this let, I cried:
'Look in my face, and if you find not there
Pledge of my truth, Heaven help me, for 't is all —
All I can give!' — 'Ah! my poor child,' said he,
'Such warrant have I learnt to take with doubt;
For I have known a face, too beautiful,
With look of innocence and shining candor,
Prove but the ambush of duplicity,
Pitiless and impure. But let me not
Distrust too far.' Then he turned up the gas,
And, with a scrutiny intent and grave,
Perused my face. "What is your name?' he asked,
After a silence. — ' Mary Merivale.'
'Well, Mary, I engage you; come at once.
In the next room asleep reclines our patient.
As for your wages, we will say two guineas
A week, if you 're content.' — 'O, perfectly!'

" So, groping in my darkness, I at length

Hit on the door that issued into light.
Long talks between the patient and his friend
Were frequent, and they heeded not my presence.
Little by little Percival soon told
The story that you 've heard, and more which you
May never hear in earthly interviews.
An eager listener, I would treasure up
Each word, each look; and on my soul at last
Dawned the pure ray by which I saw those traits,
The spirit's own, that harmonized so well
With all the outward showed of good and noble.
Strange that he took no notice of the way
My very life was drifting! But to him
I seemed a child, and his paternal airs
Froze me and checked.
    "A paragraph, 'The Times'
Had published, when the accident took place,
Mentioned that Kenrick was a millionnaire,
Though quite a young man still.
     "A month went by

And he was able to sit up awhile ;
And soon, with me beside him in the carriage,
To take a drive ; — when one day, Percival
Said to me : 'Mary, you and I must try
The span to-day ; our patient shall keep house.'
My heart beat wildly ; Kenrick looked as if
Approving the arrangement ; so we went.
'I wished,' said Percival, 'to talk with you
In private ; do not answer if I put
Questions that may embarrass or annoy ;
It is no idle curiosity,
Prompting me now. We see that you were born
To something better than this drudgery :
If not reluctant, tell me who you are.'
'O, willingly !' I said.

      "And so I told him
All, from the first. He heard me patiently ;
And then remarked : 'But do you never long
For that secure and easy life at home ?
You will go back to Liverpool, perchance,

When you 've had quite enough of servitude
And toil precarious.' — 'I go not back,'
Said I, 'while health and liberty are left.
The home that 's grudged is not the home for me.
Give me but love, and like the reed I yield;
Deal with me harshly, you may break, not bend
    me.'
'Ah! there is something wrong in all these
    things,'
Replied he, musing.
                "'Yes,' I said; 'consider
What I 've been telling of my mother's way
Of marrying her daughters; well, my mother
Is but the product of that social system,
Hollow and false, which leaves for dowerless girls
Few honorable outlooks for support
Excepting marriage. Poor, dependent, helpless,
Untaught in any craft that could be made
To yield emolument, — our average women, —
What can they do but take the common path

Which my poor mother would have made *me* try,
And lead some honest man to think that they
Are wedding *him*, and not his bank-account?
Let woman, equally with man, be bred
To learn with thoroughness some craft or trade
By which she may support herself at least,
You place her more at liberty to shun
Unions, no priest, no church can sanctify!'

"Percival eyed me with a puzzled look,
Then said: 'The time is on its way, I hope,
When from her thraldom woman will come forth,
And in her own hands take her own redress;
When laws disabling her shall not be made
Under the cowardly, untested plea
That man is better qualified than woman
To estimate her needs and do her justice.
Justice to her shall be to man advancement;
And woman's wit can best heal woman's wrongs.
Accelerate that time, all women true

To their own sex, — yet not so much to that
As to themselves and all the human race!
But pardon me; I wander from the point, —
Following you. Now tell me, could you make
America your home?'

"The sudden question
Made my heart leap, and the hot crimson rush
Up to my brow. Silent I bowed my head,
And he continued thus: 'If it should be,
That one, not wholly alien to your tastes, —
A man not quite so young as you, perhaps,
But not beyond his prime, — an honest man, —
I will not say with ample means, for that
Would jar upon your heart, — one who could
    make
Your home a plentiful and happy one, —
Should offer you his hand, — would it deter you
To know that in America your lot
Must henceforth be?'

"My breath came quick, — my eyes

Turned swift away, lest he should mark their joy
And count his prize too cheaply won.   I sighed,
But did not speak. 'May I go on?' he asked.
A 'yes' distinct, though faint, flew from my lips.
'May I,' said he, 'tell Kenrick he may hope?'
'What!' cried I, looking up, with something fiercer
Than mere chagrin in my unguarded frown."

Linda broke in upon the story here,
And turning to her father with a smile
Tender as dawning light, yet arch and gay,
Cried, "Fie, my father! Could you be so dull?
How could you treat my future mother so?"
"Nay, do not blame me hastily," said he,
With glad paternal eyes regarding her;
"How could a modest man — and I was one —
Suppose that youth and wealth, and gracious gifts
Of person, such as Kenrick wore so well,

Could fail to win? Truly I did not dream,
Spite of the proverb, Love could be so blind."

Tossing her head with mock vindictive air,
Like sweet sixteen, the mother then resumed:
"Kenrick, it seems, being a bashful man, —
And somewhat shy, perhaps, because I knew
He was but recently in mad pursuit
Of an unfaithful spouse, a runaway,
Commissioned Percival to try the ground,
Obscure and doubtful, of my woman's will.
My absolute 'What!' was unequivocal.
Then turning to the coachman, Percival,
Said, 'Home, now, home! and quickly!'

                                   "Home we rattled,
And both were silent to our journey's end.
An eager glance he gave me as he touched
My hand to help me from the carriage. He
Has told me since that I returned the look
With one which, if not actually scorn,

Was next of kin to scorn, and much resem-
    bling: —
All the chimera of his guilty conscience.

" Kenrick next day renewed his suit by letter ;
He begged I would not give a hasty ' No,'
But wait and grant him opportunities
To prove that he was worthy and sincere,
And to procure the requisite divorce.
While I was answering his letter, he
Drove out with Percival. My brief reply
Told him there could be no decision other
Than a complete and final negative.

" Then I sat down and ran my fingers over
The keys of the piano ; and my mood
At length expressed itself in that wild burst
Of a melodious anguish, which Edgardo
Gives vent to in ' Lucia.' Words could add
Nothing to magnify the utter heart-break

Of that despair ; and Donizetti's score
Has made the cry audible through the ages.
Less from the instrument than from my heart
Was wrung the passionate music.

       "At its close,
A long-drawn breath made me look round, and
  there
Whom should I see but Percival, as if
Transfixed in mute surprise! 'I did not know
There was a listener, — had supposed you gone,'
Said I ; and he replied : 'I thought you 'd have
Some word for Kenrick : so our drive was short.'
'Nothing but this.' I handed him my letter ;
He took it, bowed, and left me.

       " The next day
I learnt that Kenrick had engaged his passage
In Wednesday's steamer for New York. My
  stay
Must now be brief ; my services no longer
Could be of any use ; and so I wrote

Some formal lines, addressed to Percival,
Asking for my dismissal, and conveying
To both the gentlemen my thanks sincere
For all their kindness and munificence.
Two days I waited, but no answer came.

"The third day Kenrick sought an interview.
We met, and freely talked of this and that.
Said he, at last: 'Into what false, false ways
We plunge because we do not care to *think!*
We shudder at Chinese morality
When it allows a parent to destroy
Superfluous female children.   Look at home!
Have we no ancient social superstitions
Born of the same old barbarous family?
My life, Miss Merivale, has been so crowded
That I've had little time to trace opinion
Down to its root before accepting it.
In giving opportunity for thought,
Sickness has been a brisk iconoclast.

Behold the world's ideal of a wife!
'T is something like to this:

      " 'She marries young,
Perhaps in meek submission to the will
Parental, or in hope of a support;
In a few years, — as heart and brain mature,
And knowledge widens, — finds her lord and
   master
Is a wrong-headed churl, a selfish tyrant,
A miser, or a blockhead, or a brute;
Her love for him, if love there ever was,
Is turned to hatred or indifference:
What shall she do? The world has one reply:
You made your bed, and you must lie in it;
True, you were heedless seventeen — no matter!
True, a false sense of duty urged you on,
And you were wrongly influenced — no matter!
Be his wife still; stand by him to the last;
Do not rebel against his cruelty;
The more he plays the ruffian, the more merit

In your endurance! Suffering is your lot;
It is the badge and jewel of a woman.
Shun not contamination from his touch;
Keep having children by him, that his traits
And his bad blood may be continuous.
Think that you love him still; and feed your
    heart
With all the lies you can, to keep it passive!

"'So say the bellwethers who lead the many
Over stone walls into the thorns and ditches,
Because their fathers took that way before them.
Such is the popular morality!
But is it moral? Nay; when man or woman
Can look up, with the heart of prayer, and say,
Forbid it, Heaven, forbid it, self-respect,
Forbid it, merciful regard for others,
That this one should be parent to my child,—
That moment should the intimate relations
Of marriage end, and a release be found!

"'How many blunder in mistaking Passion,
Mixed with a little sentiment, for Love!
Passion may lead to Love, as it may lead
Away from Love, but Passion is not Love;
It may exist with Hate; too often leads
Its victim blindfold into hateful bonds,
Under the wild delusion that Love leads.
Love's bonds are adamant, and Love a slave;
And yet Love's service must be perfect freedom.
Candor it craves, for Love is innocent, —
But no enforced fidelity, no ties
Such as the harem shelters. Dupes are they
Who think that Love can ever be compelled!
Only what's lovely Love can truly love,
And fickleness and falsehood are deformed.
Reveal their features, Love may mourn indeed,
But will not rave. Love, even when abandoned,
Feels pity and not anger for the heart
That could not prize Love's warm fidelity.
But Passion, selfish, proud, and murderous,

Seizes the pistol or the knife, and kills; —
And cozened juries make a heroine
Of her who, stung with jealousy or pride,
Or, by some meaner motive, hurled a wreck,
Assassinates her too inconstant wooer.

"'Now do I see how little, in my case,
There was of actual love, how much of passion!
Love's day for me, if it may ever come
In this brief stage, is yet to dawn. You smile;
Love must have hope, a ray of hope, at least,
To catch the hue of life; and so, Miss Mary,
I'll not profess to love you; all I say
Is, that a little hope from you would make me!
But, since we can't be lovers, let's be friends;
Here, in this little wallet, is a check
For an amount that will secure your future
From serious want, — a sum I shall not miss.
But which —'
   "With many thanks I answered 'No!'

'What can I do?' he asked, 'to show my debt
To you and Percival?' I shook my head,
And something in the sadness of my smile
Arrested his attention. But that moment
A girl rushed in with cry of 'O, he 's killed —
Killed, the poor man!' — 'Who?' — 'Mr. Per-
    cival!'
The name was like a blow upon my heart,
And Kenrick saw it, and supported me.

"But in a moment I was strong. I heard
A scuffling noise of people at the door,
And then a form — 't was Percival's — was borne
Into a room, and placed upon a bed.
Pale and insensible he lay; a surgeon
Came in; at last we got an explanation:
In rescuing from a frightened horse the child
Of a poor woman, Percival had been
Thrown down, an arm been broken, and the pain
Had made him faint. My nervous laugh of joy,

When I was sure that this was the extreme
Of injury, betrayed my reckless heart,
And Kenrick had my secret.   Percival
Was soon himself; the broken limb was set,
And I, engaged to stay another week
To wait on the new patient — nothing loath.

"The day of his departure, Kenrick drew me
Aside, and, in a whisper, said, 'He loves you!'
'Loves me?'   With palms held tightly on my
  breast
To keep my heart down, I repeated, 'Loves
  me?'
'T was hard to credit.   'Pardon me,' said Ken-
  rick,
'If by communication of your secret,
I changed the desolation of his life
To sudden bloom and fragrance, for a moment.'
'A moment only?' — 'Soon his scruples rose:
It cannot be! he said; two mountains lie

Between my fate and hers. — Two bubbles rather!
Retorted I; let's take their altitude. —
One is my age. — That mountain is already
Tunnelled or levelled, since she sees it not. —
The other is that infamous decree
Against me at the period of my suit,
Granting the guilty party a divorce,
But me prohibiting to wed again. —
Well, that decree (I answered bitterly)
Would have with me the weight of a request
That I'd hereafter quaff at common puddles
And not at one pure fount; I'd heed the bar
As I would heed the grass-webbed gossamer;
I'd sooner balk a bench of drivellers
Than outrage sacred nature. — If that bench
Could have you up for bigamy, what then? —
The dear old dames! they should not have the
   means
To prove it on me: for the pact should be
'Twixt me and her who would accept my troth

Freely before high heaven and all its angels:
Witnesses which the sheriff could not summon,
Could not, at least, produce. — But, Kenrick, you
Do not consider all the risk and pain;
The social stigma, and, should children come,
The grief, the shame, the disrepute to them. —
To which I answered: God's great gift of life,
Coming through parentage select and pure,
To me is such a sacred, sacred thing,
So precious, so inestimably precious,
That your objections seem of small account;
Since only stunted hearts and slavish minds
Could visit on your children disrepute,
Who fitly could ignore such Brahmanism,
Since they 'd be born, most probably, with brains.

"'When the neglect of form, if 't is neglected,
Is all in honor, purged of selfishness,
Where shall the heart and reason lay the blame?
But understand me: Would I cheapen form?

Nay, I should fear that those who would evade it,
Without a reason potent as your own,
Trifled with danger. But I cannot make
A god of form, an idol crushing me.
Unlike the church, I look on marriage as
A civil contract, not a sacrament,
Indissoluble, spite of every wrong;
The high and holy purposes of marriage
Are not fulfilled in instances where each
Helps to demoralize or blight the other;
Let it then stand, like other contracts, on
A basis purely personal and legal.

"'Oh! how we hug the fictions we are born to!
Challenging never, never testing them;
Accepting them as irreversible;
Part of God's order, not to be improved;
Placing the form above the informing spirit,
The outward show above the inward life;
A hollow lie, well varnished, well played out,

Above the pure, the everlasting truth;
Fancying Nature is not Nature still,
Because repressed, or cheated, or concealed;
Juggling ourselves with frauds a very child,
Yet unperverted, readily would pierce!

"'Consider my own case: a month ago,
See me a maniac, rushing forth to find
A wife who loved me not; my heart all swollen
With rage against the man to whom I owed
Exposure of her falsehood; ah, how blind!
To chase a form from which the soul had fled!
If I grew sane at length, you, Percival,
And the mere presence of our little nurse
Have brought me light and healing. I am cured,
Thank Heaven, and can exult at my release.

"'Here I paused. Percival made no reply,
But sat like one absorbed. I paced the floor
Awhile, and then confronting him resumed:—

Your scruples daunt you still; well, there 's a way
To free you from the meshes of the law:
On my return, I 'll go to Albany,
Where war's financial sinews, as you know,
Are those of legislation equally;
I 'll have a law put through to meet your case;
To strip away these toils.   I can; I will! —
Percival almost stunned me with his No!
Make *me* a gutter, adding more pollution
To the fount of public justice?   Never!   No!
I would not feed corruption with a bribe,
To win release to-morrow.   Such a cure
Would be, my friend, far worse than the disease. —
Then there 's no way, said I; and so, farewell!
The carriage waits to take me to the station. —
I shall not say farewell until we part
Beside the carriage-door, said he: you 'll take
Your leave of Mary? — Yes, I go to seek her. —
And this, Miss Mary, is a full report
Of all that passed between my friend and me.'

"Here Kenrick ended. He had been, methought,
Thus copious, in the hope his argument
Would make me look as scornfully as he
On obstacles that Percival would raise.
I thanked him for his courtesy, and then,
Not without some emotion, we two parted.
When the last sound of the retiring wheels
Was drowned in other noises, Percival
Came in, and found me waiting in the parlor.
' Now let me have a talk with you,' he said.
So, in the little parlor we sat down.
I see it now, all vividly before me!
The carpet — ay, its very hues and figures :
The chandelier, the sofa, the engraving
Of Wellington that hung above the mantel;
The little bookcase, holding Scott and Irving,
And Gibbon's Rome, and Eloisa's Letters ;
And, in a vase, upon the marble stand,
An opening rose-bud I had plucked that day —
Type of my own unfolding, rosy hope!

"Said Percival: 'We'll not amuse each other
With words indifferent; and we'll allow
Small opportunity for hearts to speak:
We know what they would utter, might we dare
To give them audience.   Let Reason rule.
What I propose is this: that we now part —
Part for two years; and when that term shall end,
If we are still in heart disposed as now,
Then can we orient ourselves anew,
And shape our course as wary conscience bids.
Till then, no meeting and no correspondence!

"'Now for conditions more particular:
You have a sister — Mrs. Hammersley —
Julia, I think you said, — an elder sister,
Resident here, and in society,
But fretted by her lord's extravagance
And her own impecuniosity.
You at her house shall be a visitor,
But not without the means of aiding her;

And who but I can now supply the means?
Here's the dilemma: how can you be free
If you're my debtor? Yet you *must* be free,
And promise to be free; nor let my gift
Sway you one jot in trammelling your heart.
Two years you'll spend with Mrs. Hammersley;
Accepting all Society can offer
To welcome youth and beauty to its lap;
Keeping your heart as open as you can
To influences and impressions new;
For, Mary, bear in mind how young you are!
So much for *you*. On *my* part, I'll return
To my own country, and endeavor there
Once more to rectify the wretched wrong
That circumscribes me. I shall fail perhaps —
But we can be prepared for either issue.'

" Here he was silent, and I said: 'You're right,
And I accept your terms without reserve.'
We parted, and except a clasp of hands

That lingered in each other, and a glance
That flashed farewell from eyes enthroning truth,
There was no outward token of our love.

"Two years (the longest of my life were they!)
Emptied their sands at last, and then I wrote
A letter to him, to the Barings' care,
Containing one word only; this: '*Unchanged.*'
In the same old familiar room we met:
Eager I gave my hand; but he drew back,
Folded his arms, and said, with half a smile:
''T is not for me; still am I under ban!'
'I 'm glad of that!' cried I; ''t will help to show
How slight, to love like mine, impediments
Injustice can pile up!'
     " He took my hand,
And, for the first time, we exchanged a kiss.
Then we sat down and freely talked. Said he:
'Baffled in all my efforts to procure
Reversal of my sentence, I resolved

The Mother's Story.

To terminate one misery at least:
Yearly the court compelled me, through my bonds-
    men,
To render an account of all my income,
Of which the larger portion must be paid
For the support of my betrayer, and
The child, called, by a legal fiction, mine.
To this annoyance of an annual dealing
With her attorney, I would put an end ;
And so I compromised by giving up
Two thirds of all my property at once.
This leaves me free from all entanglement
With her or hers, — though with diminished
    means.

"' And now, since still you venture to confide
Wholly in me, my Mary Merivale, —
And since you would intrust your happiness
To one who can but give you love for love, —
To make our income certain, 't is my plan

Straightway my little remnant to convert
Into a joint annuity, to last
During our natural lives: this will secure
A fair, though not munificent support.
And since for me you put the gay world by,
And since for you I make no sacrifice,
Now shape our way of life as you may choose.'

"This I disclaimed; but we at last arranged
That on the morrow, in the presence of
My poor friend Lucy, and my sister Julia,
We two should take each other by the hand
As emblem of a pledge including all
Of sacred and inviolable, all
Of holy and sincere, that man and woman,
Uniting for connubial purposes,
And with no purpose foreign to right love,
Can, with responsible intelligence,
Give to each other in the face of God,
And before human witnesses.

"And so
The simple rite — if such it could be called —
Took place. A formal kiss was interchanged,
And then we all knelt down, and Percival
Met our hearts' need with such a simple prayer
As by its quickening and inspiring faith
Made us forget it was another's voice,
Not our own hearts, that spoke. My sister Julia
Wept, not for me, but for herself, poor child!
The chill, the gloom of an unhappy future
Crept on her lot already, like a mist
Foreshadowing the storm; she saw, not distant,
All the despair of a regretful marriage
Menacing her and driving forth her children.
It did not long delay. Her spendthrift lord,
After a squander of his own estate,
And after swindling my confiding father
Of a large sum, deserted wife and children,
To play the chevalier of industry
At Baden, or at Homburg, and put on

More of the aspect of the beast each day.
Three children have his blood to strive against.
Poor Julia! What she has to live on now
Was given by Linda's father. We found means,
Also, to set up our poor sewing-girl,
My old companion, Lucy, in a trade
In which she thrives, — she and a worthy husband.

.

"What said my parents? Well, I wrote them soon,
Relating all the facts without reserve,
And asking, 'Would it be agreeable to them
To have a visit from us?' They replied,
'It will not be agreeable, for our house
Is one of good repute.' — Not three years after,
A joint appeal came to us for their aid
To the amount of seven hundred pounds.
We sent the money, and it helped to smooth
Their latter days; perhaps to mitigate

The anger they had felt; and yet not they:
Of the ungenerous words addressed to us
My father never knew.

      "We met my sisters,
Through Julia's urging, I believe, and proudly
I let them see what sort of man I 'd chosen.
We travelled for a time in England; then,
In travel and in study, spent three years
Upon the Continent; and sailed at last
For the great land to which my thoughts had
  turned
So often — for America. Arriving
Here in New York, we took this little house,
Scene of so many joys and one great woe;
And yet a woe so full of heavenly life
We should not call it by a mournful name.

"At length our Linda came to make all bright;
And I can say, should the great summoner
Call me this day to leave you, liberal Heaven

More than my share of mortal bliss already
Would have bestowed.   Yes, little Linda came!
To spoil us for all happiness but that
In which she too could share — the dear beguiler!
And with the sceptre of her love she ruled us,
And with a happy spirit's charm she charmed us,
Artfully conquering by shunning conquest,
And by obeying making us obey.
And so, one day, one happy day in June,
We all sat down together, and her mother
Told her the story which here terminates."

IV.

PARADISE FOUND.

"You might have made it longer," murmured
    Linda,
Who with moist eyes had listened, and to whom
The time had seemed inexplicably brief.
Then with an arm round either parent's neck,
And with a kiss on either parent's cheek,
She said : " My lot is as the good God gave it ;
And I'd not have it other than it is.
Could a permit from any human lips
Have made me any more a child of God?

Have made me any more your child, my parents?
Have made me any more my own true self?
Happy, and oh! not diffident to feel
My right to be and breathe the common air?
Could any form of words approving it
Have made us three more intimately near?
Have made us three more exquisitely dear?
Ah! if it could, our love is not the love
I hold it now to be — immortal love!"

With speechless joy and a new pride they gazed
Into her fair and youthful countenance,
Bright with ethereal bloom and tenderness.
Then smoothing back her hair, the father said:
"An anxious thought comes to us now and
    then, —
Comes like a cloud: the thought that we as yet
Have no provision from our income saved
For Linda. My few little ventures, made
In commerce, in a profitable hope,

So adversely resulted that I saw
My best advance would be in standing still.
As you have heard, all that we now possess
Is in a life-annuity which ends
With two frail lives — your mother's and my own.
So, should death overtake us both at once, —
And this I've looked on as improbable, —
Our little girl would be left destitute."

"Not destitute, my father!" Linda cried;
"Far back as thought can go, you taught me
    this:
To help myself; to seek, in my own mind,
Companionship forever new and glad,
Through studies, meditations, and resources
Which nature, books, and crowded life supply:
And then you urged me to excel in something;
('Better do one thing thoroughly,' you said,
'Than fifty only tolerably well,') —
Something from which, with loving diligence,

I might, should life's contingencies require,
Wring a support ; — and then, how carefully
You taught me how to deal with slippery men!
Taught me my rights, the laws, the very forms
By which to guard against neglect or fraud
In any business — till I 'm half a lawyer.
You taught me, too, how to protect myself,
Should force assail me ; how to hold a pistol,
Carry it, fire it — Heaven save me from the need!
And, when I was a very little girl,
You used to take me round to see the houses
As they were built ; the clearing of the land ;
The digging of the cellar ; the foundations ;
You told me that the sand to make the mortar
Ought to be fresh, and not the sea-shore sand ;
Else would the salt keep up a certain moisture.
And then we 'd watch the framework, and the
   roofing ;
And you 'd explain the office and the name
Of every beam, and make me understand

The qualities of wood, seasoning of timber,
And how the masons, and the carpenters,
The plasterers, the plumbers, and the slaters,
Should do their work; and when they slighted
 it,
And when the wood-work was too near the flue,
The flue too narrow, or the draught defective:
So that, as you yourself have often said,
I'm better qualified than half the builders
To plan and build a house, and guard myself
From being cheated in the operation.
Fear not for me, my parents; spend your income
Without a thought of saving. And besides,
Had you not trained me aptly as you have,
Am I not better — I — than many sparrows?
There is a heavenly Father over all!"

"Sweet arguer!" said Percival, "may He
And his swift angels love and help our Linda!
Your mother and myself have tried of late

To study how and where we might reduce
Certain expenses that have been, ——"

                                        But here
The dinner-bell broke in; and lighter thoughts —
Thoughts that but skim the surface of the mind,
And stir not its profound — were interchanged
As now more timely; for the Percivals
Lacked not good appetites, and every meal
Had its best stimulant in cheerfulness.
"Where shall we go to pass our holidays?"
The mother asked: "August will soon be here."
"What says our Linda?" answered Percival:
"The seaside or the mountains shall it be?"
"Linda will go with the majority!
You've spilt the salt, papa; please throw a little
Over your shoulder; there! that saves a quarrel.
To me you leave it, do you? to decide
Where we shall go? Then hear the voice of
        wisdom:
The mountain air is good, I love the mountains;

And the sea air is good, I love the sea;
But if you two prefer the mountain air,—
Go to the mountains. On the contrary,—"
"She's neutral!" cried the father; "what a
    dodger
This little girl has grown! Come, now, I'll cast
Into the scale my sword, and say we'll go
To old Cape Ann. Does any slave object?
None. 'T is a special edict. Pass the peas.
Our rendezvous shall be off Eastern Point.
There shall our Linda try the oar again."

Dinner was ended, and the gas was lit,
And The Day's last edition had been put
Into his hand to read, when suddenly
Turning to Mary, with a sigh he said:
"Kenrick, I see, is dead — Kenrick, our friend.
'Died in Chicago on the seventh instant,—
Leaves an estate valued at seven millions.'"
"Indeed! our faithful Kenrick — is he dead?

Leaves he a wife?"—"Probably not, my dear;
Three months ago he was a single man;
I had a letter from him, begging me,
If I lacked funds at any time to draw
On him, and not be modest in my draft."
"But that was generous; what did you reply?"
"I thanked him for his love, and promised him
He should be first to hear of wants of mine.
Now let us to the music-room adjourn,
And hear what will not jar with our regrets."
They went; and Mary mother played and sang;
Played the 'Dead March in Saul' and sang 'Old
  Hundred,'
'Come, ye Disconsolate,' 'When thee I seek'—
And finally these unfamiliar words:—

I.

O, give me one breath from that land —
 The land to which all of us go!
Even now, O my soul! art thou fanned
 By the breezes that over it blow.

II.

By the breezes that over it blow!
   Though far from the knowledge of sense,
The shore of that land thou dost know —
   There soon wilt thou go with me hence.

III.

There soon wilt thou go with me hence —
   But where, O my soul! where to be?
In that region, that region immense,
   The loved and the lost shall we see?

IV.

The loved and the lost shall we see!
   For Love all it loves shall make near;
Type and outcome of Love shall it be —
   Our home in that infinite sphere!

A day's excursion to a favorite spot —
Choice nook among the choicest of Long Island,
(Paradise Found, he called it playfully) —
Had oft been planned; and one day Percival
Said: "Let us go to day!" — "No, not to-day!"
Cried Linda, with a shudder. — "And why not?

It is the very day of all the year!
There's an elastic coolness in the air,
Thanks to the thunder-shower we had last night:
A day for out-of-doors! Your reasons, Linda?
Tears in your eyes! Nay, I'll not ask for reasons.
We will not go." — "Yes, father, let us go.
Whence came my No abrupt, I could not say;
It was a sudden freak, and what it meant
You know as well as I. Shall we get ready?"
"Ay, such a perfect day is rare; it seems
To bring heaven nearer to my understanding;
Life, life itself is joy enough! to be, —
To breathe this ether, see that arch of blue,
Is happiness." — "But 't is the soul that makes it;
What would it be, my father, without love?"
"Ay, without love, love human and divine,
No atmosphere of real joy can be."

Not long the time mother and daughter needed
To don their simple, neat habiliments.

A postman handed Percival a letter
As they descended from the door to take
The carriage that would bear them to the station;
For they must go by rail some twenty miles
To reach this paradise of Percival's.

When they were in the cars, and these in motion,
Percival drew the letter from his pocket,
And, while he read, a strange expression stole
Over his features. "Now what is it, father?"
Then with a sigh which her quick ear detected
As one that masked a pleasurable thought,
He said: "Poor little Linda!"—"And why
    poor?"
"Because she will not be so rich again
In wishes unfulfilled. That grand piano
You saw at Chickering's—what was the price?"
"Twelve hundred dollars only."—"It is yours!
That painting you admired so—that by Church—
What did they ask for it?"—"Two thousand
    dollars."

"'T is cheap at that. We'll take it. Whose turn-
    out
Was it that struck your fancy?" — "Miss Van
    Hagen's!"
"Well, you shall have one like it, only better.
Look! What a charming cottage! How it stands,
Fronting the water, flanked by woods and gar-
    dens!
For sale, I see. We'll buy it. No, that house
Yonder upon the hill would suit us better;
Our coachman's family shall have the cottage."

"What is it all, my father? You perplex me,"
Said Linda, with a smile of anxious wonder.
"In brief, my little girl," said Percival,
"You're grown to be an heiress. Let your mother
Take in that letter. Read it to her, Linda."
It was a letter from executors
Of the late Arthur Kenrick, making known
That in his several large bequests was one
Of a full million, all to Percival.

The mother's heart flew to the loved ones gone;
She sighed, but not to have them back again;
That were a wish too selfish and profane.
And then, the first surprise at length allayed,
Calmly, but not without a natural joy
At being thus lifted to an affluent lot,
The three discussed their future. Should they travel?
Or should they choose some rural site, and build?
Paradise Found would furnish a good site!
Now they could help how many! Not aloof
From scenes of destitution had they kept:
What joy to aid the worthy poor! To save
This one from beggary! To give the means
To that forsaken widow, overworked,
With her persistent cough, to make a trip,
She and her children, city-pinched and pale,
To some good inland farm, and there recruit!
Many the plans for others they conceived!
Many the joyful —

Ah! a shivering crash!
A whirl of splintered wood and loosened iron!
Then shrieks and groans of pain . . . .
A broken rail
Had done it all. Now for the killed and wounded!
Ghastly the spectacle! And happy those
Whom Death had taken swiftly! Linda's mother
Was one of these — a smile upon her lips,
But her breast marred — peacefully she had
    passed.
Percival's wound was mortal, but he strove,
Amid the jar of sense, to fix his mind
On one absorbing thought — a thought for Linda:
For she, though stunned, they told him, would
    survive,
Motherless, though — soon to be fatherless!
And something — ah! what was it? — must be
    done,
Done, too, at once. "O gentlemen, come here!
Paper and pen and ink! Quick, quick, I pray
    you!

No matter ! Come ! A pencil — that will do.
Help me to make a will — I do bequeathe —
Where am I ? What has happened ? God be
    with me !
Yes, I remember now — the will ! the will !
No matter for the writing ! Witness ye
That I bequeathe, convey, and hereby give
To this my only child, named Linda — Linda —
God ! What's my name ? Where was I ? Per-
    cival
To Linda Percival — Is this a dream ?
What would I do ? My heart is drowned in blood.
God help me. Linda — Linda ! "
                              Then he died ;
And, chasing from his face that glare of anguish,
Came a smile beatific as if angels
Had soothed his fears and hushed him into calm.

Her father's cry was all unheard by Linda,
Or by her mortal senses all unheard.

Perhaps a finer faculty, removed
From the external consciousness afar,
Took it all in; for when she woke at last
To outward life, and looking round beheld
No sign of either parent, she sank back
Into a trance, and lay insensible
For many hours. Then rallying she once more
Seemed conscious; and observing the kind looks
Of an old woman and a man whose brow
Of thought contrasted with his face of youth,
She calmly said: "Don't fear to tell me all;
I think I know it all; an accident
With loss of life; my father and my mother
Among — among the killed. Enough! Your
    silence
Explains it now. So leave me for a while.
Should I need help, I'll call. You're very good."

When they returned, Linda was sitting up
Against the pillow of the bed; her hands

Folded upon her breast; her open eyes
Tearless and glazed, as if celestial scenes,
Clear to the inner, nulled the outer vision.
The man drew near, touched her upon the brow,
And said, "My name is Henry Meredith."
She started, and, as on an April sky
A cloud is riven, and through the sudden cleft
The sunshine darts, even so were Linda's eyes
Flooded with conscious lustre, and she woke.

It was a neatly furnished cottage room
In which she lay, and nodding eglantine,
With its sweet-scented foliage and rath roses,
Rustled and shimmered at the open window.
"How long have I been lying here?" asked Linda.
"Almost two days," said Meredith. — "Indeed!
I read, sir, what you'd ask me, in your looks;
And to the question on your mind I answer,

If all is ready, let the funeral be
This afternoon. Ay, in the village ground
Let their remains be laid. The services
May be as is convenient." "Of what faith
Were they?"— "The faith of Christ."— "But
    that is vague.
The faith of Christ? Mean you the faith *in*
    Christ?
Faith in the power and need of his atonement?"

"All that I mean is, that they held the faith
Which was the faith of Christ, as manifest
In his own words, unwrenched by others' words.
So to no sect did they attach themselves;
But from all sects drew all the truth they could
In charity; believing that when Christ
Said of the pure in heart, 'They shall see God,'
He meant it; spoke no fragment of a truth;
Deferred no saying, qualifying that;
Set no word-trap for unsuspecting souls;

Spoke no oracular, ambiguous phrase,
Intending merely the vicarious pure;
Reserved no strange or mystical condition
To breed fine points of doctrine, or confound
The simple-minded and the slow of faith.
Heart-purity and singleness and love,
Fertile in loving acts, sole proof of these,
Summed up for them, my father and my mother,
All nobleness, all duty, all salvation,
And all religion."

      With a heavy sigh
Meredith turned away. "I'll not discuss
Things of such moment now," said he. "One rock,
One only rock, amid the clashing waves
Of human error, have I found, — the rock
On which Christ built his Church. Heaven show you it!"

"Heaven show me truth! let it be on the rock,
Or in the sand. You'll say Amen to that?"

"I say Amen to what the Church approves,
For I myself am weak and fallible,
Depraved by nature, reprobate and doomed,
And ransomed only by the atoning blood
Of a Redeemer more divine than human.
But controversy is not timely now:
The papers, jewels, money, and what clothes
Could properly be taken, you will find
In a small trunk of which this is the key.
At three o'clock the carriage will be ready."

Linda put forth her hand; he gravely took it,
And holding it in both of his the while,
Said: "Should you lack a friend, remember me.
I was a witness to your father's death.
Your mother must have died without a pang.
He, by a strenuous will, kept death at bay
A minute, and his dying cry was Linda!
Hardly can he have felt his sufferings,
Such the intentness of his thought for you!"

The fount of tears was happily struck at last,
And Linda wept profusely. Meredith
Quitted the room ; but the old woman sat
Beside the bed, her thin and shrunken fingers
Hiding themselves in Linda's locks of gold,
Or with a soothing motion parting them
From a brow fine and white as alabaster.
At length, like a retreating thunder-storm,
The sobs grew faint and fainter, and then ceased.

After a pause, said Linda to the lady,
"Is he your grandson ?" — "Ay, my only one ;
A noble youth, heir to a splendid fortune ;
A scholar, too, and such a gentleman !
Young ; ay, not twenty-four ! What a career,
Would he but choose ! Society is his,
To cull from as he would. He throws by all,
To be a poor tame priest, and take confessions
Of petty scandals and delinquencies
From a few Irish hussies and old women !"

"We all," said Linda, "hear the voice of duty
In different ways, and many not at all.
Honor to him who heeds the sacred claim
At any cost of life's amenities
And tenderest ties! We see the sacrifice;—
We cannot reckon up the nobleness
It called for, and must call for to the end."

V.

LINDA.

THE news of the great railroad accident
    And of the sudden death of Percival,
Coming so soon upon intelligence
Of his rare fortune in the legacy
From Kenrick, occupied the public mind
For a full day at least, and then was whelmed
In other marvels rushing thick upon it.
The mother and the daughter, who still bore
The name of Percival, came back from Paris

At once, on getting the unlooked-for news.
When Linda, after three weeks had elapsed,
Re-entered, with a swelling heart, the house
To her so full of sacred memories,
She was accosted by an officer
Who told her he had put his seal on all
The papers, plate, and jewelry belonging
To the late Albert Percival, — and asked
If in her keeping were a watch and ring,
Also some money, found upon his person:
If so, would she please give them up, and he,
Who had authority to take them, would
Sign a receipt for all such property,
And then the rightful heir could easily
Dispose of it, as might seem best to her.

"The rightful heir?" gasped Linda, taking in
Not readily the meaning of the words, —
"Do you not know that I 'm the rightful heir
And only child of Albert Percival?"

"Pardon me," said the officer, "the child,
Recognized by the law, is not yourself,
But Harriet Percival, the only heir, —
For so the court adjudges, — and to her
All property, both personal and real,
Must be made over. She, no doubt, will deal
Kindly in your peculiar case, and make
A suitable provision — "

                        "Hold!" cried Linda,
Her nostrils' action showing generous blood
As clearly as some matchless courser shows it
After a mighty race, — "Your business,
But not your comments! And yet, pardon me —
I'm hasty, — you meant well; but you would
    have me
Render you up the watch and pocket-book
Found on my father's person, and delivered
To me his daughter. That I'll only do,
When more authority than you have shown
Compels me, and my lawyer bids me yield."

"Here is my warrant," said the officer,
"And my instructions are explicit." Then,
The spirit of the gentleman disdaining
The action he was sent for, he rejoined:
"But the law's letter shall not make me do
An incivility, perhaps a wrong.
And so, relying on your truth, I leave you,
Assured that you 'll be ready to respond
To all the law can ask. And now, good day!"

Left to her own decisions, Linda sought
At once the best advice; and such had been
Her training, that she was not ignorant
Who among counsellors were trusted most
In special ways. Kindly and patiently
Her case was taken up and thoroughly
Sifted and tried. No hope! No flaw! No case!
So craftily had every step been taken,
With such precaution and such legal care, —
So diligently had the mesh been woven,

Enclosing Percival and all of his, —
That nothing could be done except put off
The payment of the Kenrick legacy
For some six months, — when it was all made
    over
To the reputed child, already rich
Through the law's disposition of the sums
Which Percival had been compelled to pay.

After the legal test, with brave composure
Linda surveyed her lot. Enough was left,
From sale of jewels that had been her mother's,
For a few months' support, with frugal care.
Claim to these jewels and the money found
Upon her mother's person had been laid
Too eagerly by the contesting party,
Who said that Percival, in dying last,
Was heir to the effects; but since the claim
Could only be upheld by proving marriage,
The claimants sorrowfully gave it up.

One day as Linda stood with folded hands
Before her easel, on which lay a painting
Of flowers autumnal, grouped with rarest skill, —
The blue-fringed gentian, the red cardinal,
With fern and plumy golden-rod intwined, —
A knock aroused her, and the opened door
Disclosed a footman, clad in livery,
Who, hat in hand, asked if a lady might
Come up to see the pictures. "Certainly,"
Was the reply; and, panting up the stairs,
A lady came whose blazonry of dress
And air of self-assured, aggressive wealth
Spoke one well pleased to awe servility.

As when by some forecasting sense the dove
Knows that the hawk, though out of sight and
    still,
Is hovering near, even so did Linda feel
An enemy draw nigh; felt that this woman,
Who, spite of marks a self-indulgent life

Leaves on the face, showed vestiges of beauty,
Was she who first had cast the bitterness
Into that cup of youth which Linda's father
Was made to taste so long.

      And yet (how strangely,
In this mixed web of life, the strands of good
Cross and inweave the evil!) to that wrong
Might he have tracked a joy surpassing hope, —
The saving angel who, in Linda's mother,
Had so enriched his being ; — might have tracked
(Mysterious thought!) Linda herself, his child,
The crown of every rapture, every hope

The lady, known as Madame Percival,
Seated herself and turned a piercing look
On Linda, who blenched not, but stood erect,
With calm and serious look regarding her.
The lady was the first to lower her eyes ;
She then, with some embarrassment, remarked:
"So! you're an artist ! Will you let me see

Some of your newest paintings?" Linda placed
Three of her choicest pieces on the easel,
And madame raised her eyeglass, looked a moment,
Said, "Very pretty," and then, breaking through
Further constraint, began: "You may not know
    me ;
My name is Percival; you, I suppose,
Bear the same name by courtesy. 'T is well:
The law at last has taught you possibly
Our relative positions. Of the past
We will say nothing; no hard thought is left
Against you in my heart; I trust I know
The meaning of forgiveness; what is due
To Christian charity. In me, although
The church has but a frail, unworthy child,
Yet would I help my enemy; remove her
From doubtful paths, and see her fitly placed
With her own kindred for protection due.
Hear my proposal now, in your behalf:
If you will go to England, where your aunts

And relatives reside, — and first will sign
A paper promising you'll not return,
And that you never will resume your suit, —
I will advance your passage-money, and
Give you five thousand dollars. Will you do it?"

The indignant No, surging in Linda's heart,
Paused as if language were too weak for it,
When, in that pause, the opening of the door
Disclosed a lady younger than the first,
Yet not unlike in features, though no blonde,
And of a figure small and delicate.
"Now, Harriet!" cried the elder of the two,
Annoyed, if not alarmed, "you promised me
You would not quit the carriage." — "Well, what
    then?
I changed my mind. Is that a thing uncommon?
Whom have we here? The name upon the door
Is Percival; and there upon the wall
I see a likeness of my father. So!

You, then, are Linda Percival! the child
For whom he could abandon me, his first!
Come, let me look at you!" — "Nay, Harriet,
This should not be. Come with me to the car-
    riage;
Come! I command you." — "Pooh! And pray,
    who cares
For your commands? I move not till I please.
We are half-sisters, Linda, but I hate you."

"Excuse me," Linda answered quietly,
"But I see no resemblance to my father
In you. Your features, form, complexion, all
Are quite unlike."—"Silence! We've had enough."
"What did she say?" cried Harriet. "Do not
    heed
A word of hers; leave her and come with me."
"She said, I bear no likeness to my father:
You heard her!" — "'T was in malice, Harriet.
Of course she would say that." — "But I must have

That photograph of him upon the wall:
'T is unlike any that I've ever seen."
And with the word she took it from the nail
And would have put it in her pocket, had not
Linda, with sudden grasp, recovered it.

Darker her dark face grew, when Harriet
Saw herself baffled; taking out her purse
She drew from it a thousand-dollar bill,
And said, "Will this procure it?" — "Harriet!
You're mad to offer such a sum as that."
"Old woman, if you anger me, you'll rue it!
I ask you, Linda Percival, if you
Will take two thousand dollars for that portrait?"
And Linda answered: "I'll not take your money:
The portrait you may have without a price;
I'm not without a copy." — "Well, I take it;
But mark you this: I shall not hate you less
For this compliance; nay, shall hate you more;
For I do hate you with a burning hatred,

And all the more for that smooth Saxon face,
With its clear red and white and Grecian outline;
That likeness to my father (I can see it),
Those golden ringlets and that rounded form.
Pray, Madame Percival, where did I get
This swarthy hue, since Linda is so fair,
And you are far from being a quadroon?
Good lady, solve the riddle, if you please."

"There! No more idle questions! Two o'clock?
That camel's hair at Stewart's will be sold,
Unless we go this minute. Such a bargain!
Come, my dear, come!" And so, cajoling, coax-
    ing,
She drew away her daughter, and the door
Closed quickly on the two. But Linda stood
In meditation rapt, as thought went back
To the dear parents who had sheltered her;
Contrasting their ingenuous love sincere
And her own filial reverence, with the scene

She just had witnessed. So absorbed she was
In visions of the past, she did not heed
The opening of the door, until a voice
Broke in upon her tender revery,
Saying, "I've come again to get your answer
To my proposal." Tranquillized, subdued
By those dear, sacred reminiscences,
Linda, with pity in her tone, replied:
"Madame, I cannot entertain your offer."
"And why not, Linda Percival?" exclaimed
The imperious lady. — "I'm not bound to give
My reasons, madame." — "Come, I'll make the sum
Ten thousand dollars." — "Money could not alter
My mind upon the subject." — "Look you, Linda;
You saw my daughter. Obstinate, self-willed,
Passionate as a wild-cat, jealous, crafty,
Reckless in use of money when her whims
Are to be gratified, and yet at times
Sordid as any miser, — she'll not stop

At artifice, or violence, or crime,
To injure one she hates — and you she hates!
Now for your sake and hers, I charge you leave
This country, go to England; — close at once
With my most liberal offer."

         "Madame, no!
This is my home, my birthplace, and the land
Of all my efforts, hopes, and aspirations;
While I have work to do, here lies my field:
I cannot quit America. Besides,
Since candor now is best, I would not take
A dole from you to save myself from starving."
The lady's eyes flashed choler. She replied:
"Go your own gait; and, when you're on the
   street,
As you'll be soon, blame no one but yourself.
I've done my part. Me no one can accuse
Of any lack of charity or care.
For three weeks more my offer shall hold good.
After that time, expect no further grace."

And, with a frown which tried to be disdain,
But which, rebuked and humbled, fell before
The pitying candor of plain Innocence,
Out of the room she swept with all her velvet.

These interviews had made our Linda feel
How quite alone in the wide world she stood.
A letter came, after her parents' death,
From her aunt, Mrs. Hammersley, requesting
A loan of fifty pounds, and telling all
The family distresses and shortcomings:
How this one's husband had proved not so rich
As was expected; how another's was
A tyrant and a niggard, so close-fisted
He parcelled out with his own hands the sugar
For kitchen use; and how another's still,
Though amply able to receive their mother,
A widow now, had yet refused to do it,
And even declined to make a contribution
For her support.   And so the gossip ran.

The picture was not pleasant. With a sigh
Not for herself, but others, Linda penned
A letter to her aunt, relating all
The events that made her powerless to aid
Her needy kinsfolk. She despatched the letter,
Then sat and thought awhile.
                            "And now for duty!"
She cried, and rose. She could not think of duty
Except as something grateful to her parents.
They were a presence so securely felt,
And so related to her every act, —
Their love was still so vigilant, so real,
That to do what, and only what, she knew
They would approve, was duty paramount;
And their approval was the smile of God!
Self-culture, work, and needful exercise, —
This was her simple summing-up of duties
Immediately before her, and to be
Fulfilled without more parleying or delay.
She found that by the labor of a month

In painting flowers from nature, she could earn
Easily sixty dollars. This she did
For two years steadily. Then came a change.
From some cause unexplained, her wild-flower sketches,
Which from their novelty and careful finish
At first had found a ready sale, were now
In less demand. Linda was not aware
That these elaborate works, to nature true,
Had been so multiplied in copies, made
By hand, or printed by the chromo art,
As to be sold at prices not one fifth
As high as the originals had cost.
Hence her own genius winged the storm and lent
The color to the cloud, that overhung
Her prospect, late so hopeful and serene.

Now came her year of struggle! Narrow means,
Discouragement, the haunting fear of debt!
One summer day, a day reminding her

Of days supremely beautiful, immortal,
(Since hallowed by undying love and joy),
A little girl, the step-child, much endeared,
Of a poor artisan who dwelt near by
On the same floor with Linda, came to her
And said: "You promised me, Miss Percival,
That some fine day you'd take me in the cars
Where I could see the grass and pluck the flowers."
"Well, Rachel Aiken, we will go to-day,
If you will get permission from your father,"
Said Linda, longing for the woodland air.
Gladly the father gave consent; and so,
Clad in her best, the little damsel sat,
While Linda filled the luncheon-box, and made
The preparations needful.

                      "What is that?"
Asked Rachel, pointing to an open drawer
In which a case of polished ebony
Glittered and caught the eye. "A pistol-case!"
"And is the pistol loaded?"—"I believe so."

"And will you take it with you?" — "Well, my
    dear,
I did not think to do so: would you have me?"
"Yes, if we 're going to the woods; for panthers
Lurk in the woods, you know." — "I 'll take it,
    Rachel;
We call this a revolver. See! Four times
I can discharge it." At a block of wood
She aimed and fired; then carefully reloaded
The piece, and put it in a hidden pocket.

Some ten miles from the city, at a place
Rich in diversity of wood and water,
They left the cars. Rachel's delight was wild.
Never was day so lovely! Never grass
So green! And O the flowers! "Look, only
    look,
Miss Percival! What is it? Can I pluck
As many as I want?" — "Ay, that 's a harebell."
"And O, look here! This red and yellow flower!

Tell me its name." — "A columbine. It grows
In clefts of rocks. That's an anemone:
We call it so because the leaves are torn
So easily by the wind; for *anemos*
Is Greek for wind." — "Oh! here's a buttercup!
I know that well. Red clover, too, I know.
Is n't the dandelion beautiful?
And O, Miss Percival, what flower is this?"
"That's a wild rose." — "What, does the rose
    grow wild?
But is not that delightful? A wild rose!
And I can take as many as I want!
I did not dream the country was so fine.
How very happy must the children be
Who live here all the time! 'T is better far
Than any garden; for, Miss Percival,
The flowers are here all free, and quite as pretty
As garden flowers. O, hark! Did ever bird
So sweetly sing?" — "That was a wood-thrush,
    dear."

"O darling wood-thrush! Do not stop so soon!
Look there, on that stone wall! What's that?"
    — "A squirrel."
Is that indeed a squirrel? Are you sure?
How I would like a nut to throw to him!
What are these little red things in the grass?"
"Wild strawberries, my dear." — "Wild straw-
    berries!
And can I eat them?" — "Yes, we'll take a plate
And pick it full, and eat them with our dinner."
"O, will not that be nice? Wild strawberries
That we have picked ourselves!"
                               And so the day
Slid on to noon; and then, it being hot,
They crossed a wall into a skirting wood,
And there sat down upon a rocky slab
Covered with dry brown needles of the pine,
And ate their dinner while the birds made music.
"'T is a free concert, ours!" said Rachel Aiken:
"How nice this dinner! What an appetite

I'm having all at once! My father says
That I must learn to eat: I soon could learn
In such a place as this! I wish my father
Himself would eat; he works too hard, I fear;
He works in lead: and the lead makes him ill.
See what nice clothes he buys me! I'm afraid
He pays for me more than he can afford,
Seeing he has a mother to support
And a blind sister; for, Miss Percival,
I'm but his step-child, and my mother died
Two years ago; then my half-sister died,
His only little girl, and now he says
That I am all he has in the wide world
To love and cherish dearly, — all his treasure.
What would I give if I could bring him here
To these sweet woods, away from lead and work!"

So the child prattled. Then, the gay dessert
Of berries being ended, Linda sat
On the rock's slope, and peeled the mosses off

Or looked up through the branches of the pines
At the sky's blue, while Rachel played around.
From tree to tree, from flower to flower, the child
Darted through leafy lanes, when, all at once,
A scream roused Linda.

      To her feet she sprang!
Instinctively (but not without a shudder)
She grasped the little pistol she had brought
At the child's prompting; from the rock ran down,
And, at a sudden bend, encountered three
Young lusty ruffians, while, a few rods off,
Another lifted Rachel in his arms,
And to the thicker wood beyond moved on.
The three stood side by side as if to bar
The path to Linda, and their looks meant mischief.
The lane was narrow. "For your life, make way!"
She cried, and raised the pistol. "No, you don't
Fool us by tricks like that!" the foremost said:

"And so, my lady —" But before the word
Was out there was a little puff of smoke,
With an explosion, not encouraging, —
And on the turf the frightened caitiff lay.
Her road now clear, reckless of torn alpaca,
Over the scattered branches Linda rushed,
Till she drew near the leader of the gang,
Who, stopping, drew a pistol with one hand,
While with the other he held Rachel fast,
Placing her as a shield before his breast.

But Linda did not waver. Dropping into
The old position that her father taught her
When to the shooting-gallery they went,
She fired. An oath, the cry of pain and rage,
Told her she had not missed her aim, — the jaw
The ruffian left exposed. One moment more,
Rachel was in her arms. Taking a path
Transverse, they hit the public road and entered
The railroad station as the train came in.

When they were safely seated, and the engine
Began to throb and pant, a sudden pallor
Spread over Linda's visage, and she veiled
Her face and fainted ; yet so quietly,
But one among the passengers observed it ;
And he came up, and taking Rachel's place
Supported Linda ; from a lady near
Borrowed some pungent salts restorative,
And finding soon the sufferer was herself,
Gave Rachel back her seat and took his own.
But at the city station, when arrived,
This gentleman came up, and bowing, said :
"Here stands my private carriage ; but to-day
I need it not. Let my man take you home."
Linda demurred. His firm will urged them in,
And she and Rachel all at once were riding
With easy bowling motion down Broadway.

The evening papers had this paragraph :
"In Baker's Woods this morning two young men

Were fired on by a female lunatic
Without a provocation, and one wounded.
The bullet was extracted. Dr. Payson,
With his accustomed skill and promptitude,
Performed the operation ; and the patient
Is doing well. We learn the unhappy woman —
She had with her a child — is still at large."
"I 'm glad it was no worse," quoth Linda, smiling.
She kissed the pistol that had been her mother's,
Wiped it, and reverently put it by.

Three summers and an autumn had rolled on
Since the catastrophe that orphaned Linda.
Midwinter with its whirling snow had come,
And, shivering through the snow-encumbered
    streets
Of the great city, men and women went,
Stooping their heads to thwart the spiteful wind.
The sleigh-bells rang, boys hooted, and policemen
Told each importunate beggar to move on.

Linda.

In a side street where Fashion late had dwelt,
But which the up-town movement now had left
A street for journeymen and small mechanics,
Dress-makers, masons, farriers, and draymen,
A female figure might be seen to enter
A lodging-house, and passing up two flights
Unlock a door that showed a small apartment
Neat, with two windows looking on the rear,
A small recess with a low, narrow bed,
A sofa, a piano, and three chairs.
'T was noon, but in the sky no cleft of blue
Flashed the soft love-light like a lifted lid.

Clad plainly was the lady we have followed, —
But with a certain grace no modiste's art
Could have contrived. Youthful she was, and yet
A gravity not pertinent to youth
Gave to her face the pathos of that look
Which a too early thoughtfulness imparts;
And this was Linda, — Linda little changed,

Though nearer by four years to womanhood
Than when we parted from her in the shadow
Of a great woe.
                    Preoccupied she seemed
Now with some painful thought, and in a slow,
Half-automatic manner she replenished
With scanty bits of coal her little stove;
Then, with a like absorbed, uncertain air,
Threw off her cloak and bonnet, and sat down;
Motionless sat awhile till she drew forth
A pocket-book, and from it took a letter,
And read these words: "You guaranteed the debt:
It now has run three months, and if to-morrow
It is not paid, we must seek legal help."
A bill of wood and coal for Rachel's father —
Some twenty dollars only! And yet Linda
Saw not the way to pay it on the morrow.
He, the poor artisan, on whose account
She had incurred the liability,
Lay prostrate with a malady, his last,

In the small room near by, with little Rachel
His only watcher. What could Linda do ?
At length, with lips compressed, and up and down
Moving her head as if to give assent
To some resolve, now fixed, she took her seat
At the piano, — from her childhood's days
So tenderly endeared, and every chord
Vibrating to some memory of her mother !
" Old friend," — she sighed ; then thought awhile
    and sang.

I.

Help me, dear chords, help me to tell in song
The grief that now must say to you Farewell !
No music like to yours can ease my heart.

II.

An infant on her knee I struck your keys,
And you made sweet my earliest lullaby :
From you I thought my requiem might come.

III.

Hard is the pang of parting, but farewell !
Harder the shame would be, if help were not ;
Go, but your tones shall thrill forevermore.

IV.

Farewell! And O my mother, dost thou hear?
Farewell! But not to thoughts forever dear.
Farewell, but not to love — but not to thee!

When little Rachel, by her father sent,
Came in to take her lesson the next day,
Behold, no instrument was in the room!
What could it mean? "We must give up," said Linda,
"Our music for a little while. Perhaps
I soon shall have my dear piano back."
Then they went in to see the sufferer.
A smile lit up his face, — a grateful smile,
That lent a beauty even to Disease,
Pale, thin, and hollow-eyed:

"Is not the air
Quite harsh to-day?" he asked. "A searching air."
"So I supposed. I find it hard to breathe.
Dear lady — but you 've been a friend indeed!

In my vest-pocket you will find a wallet.
All that I have is in it. Take and use it.
A fellow-workman brought me yesterday
Fifty-two dollars, by my friends subscribed:
Take from it what will pay for coal and rent.
To-morrow some one of my friends will come
To see to what the morrow may require.
You 've done so much, dear lady, I refrain
From asking more." — " Ask all that you would
    have."
" My little Rachel — she will be alone,
All, all alone in this wide, striving world:
An orphan child without a relative!
Could you make interest to have her placed
In some asylum ? " — " Do not doubt my zeal
Or my ability to have it done.
And should good fortune come to me, be sure
Rachel shall have a pleasant home in mine."
" That 's best of all. Thank you. God help you
    both.

Now, Rachel, say the little prayer I taught you.
. . . That was well said. Now kiss me for good
    night.
That's a dear little girl! I'll tell your mother
How good and diligent and kind you are;
How careful, too, of all your pretty clothes;
And what a nurse you've been, — how true and
    tender.
Rachel, obey Miss Percival. Be quick
To shun all evil. Fly from heedless play-
    mates.
Close your young eyes on all impurity.
Cast out all naughty thoughts by holy prayer.
Love only what is good. Ah! darling child,
I hoped to shield you up to womanhood,
But God ordains it otherwise. May He
Amid the world's thick perils be your Guide!
There! Do not cry, my darling. All is well.
Sing us some pious hymn, Miss Percival."
And Linda, with wet eyelids, sang these words.

I.

Be of good cheer, O Soul!
    Angels are nigh;
Evil can harm thee not,
    God hears thy cry.

II.

Into no void shalt thou
    Spring from this clay;
His everlasting arm
    Shall be thy stay.

III.

Day hides the stars from thee,
    Sense hides the heaven
Waiting the contrite soul
    That here has striven.

IV.

Soon shall the glory dawn
    Making earth dim;
Be not disquieted,
    Trust thou in Him!

" O, thank you! Every word is true — I know it.
Sense hides it now, but has not always hid.

Remember, Rachel, that I say it here,
Weighing my words: I know it all is true.
God bless you both. I 'm very, very happy.
My pain is almost gone. I 'll sleep awhile."
Rachel and Linda sat an hour beside him,
Silently watching. Linda then arose
And placed her hand above his heart: 't was still.
Tranquilly as the day-flower shuts its leaves
And renders up its fragrance to the air,
From the closed mortal senses had he risen.

One day the tempter sat at Linda's ear:
Sat and discoursed — so piously! so wisely!
She held a letter in her hand; a letter
Signed Jonas Fletcher. Jonas was her landlord;
A man of forty — ay, a gentleman;
Kind to his tenants, liberal, forbearing;
Rich and retired from active business;
A member of the Church, but tolerant;

A man sincere, cordial, without a flaw
In habits or in general character;
Of comely person, too, and cheerful presence.
Long had he looked on Linda, and at last
Had studied her intently; knew her ways,
Her daily occupations; whom she saw,
And where she went. He had an interest
Beyond that of the landlord, in his knowledge;
The letter was an offer of his hand.
Of Linda's parentage and history
He nothing knew, and nothing sought to know.
He took her as she was; was well content,
With what he knew, to run all other risks.
The letter was a good one and a frank;
It came to Linda in her pinch of want,
Discouragement, and utter self-distrust.
And thus the tempter spoke and she replied:

"You're getting thin; you find success in art
Is not a thing so easy as you fancied.

Five years you've worked at what you modestly
Esteem your specialty. Your specialty!
As if a woman could have more than one, —
And that — maternity! I do not speak
Of the six years you gave your art before
You strove to make it pay. Methinks you see
Your efforts are a failure. What's the end
Of all your toil? Not enough money saved
For the redemption of your pawned piano!
Truly a cheerful prospect is before you :
To hear your views would edify me greatly."

"Yes, I am thinner than I was ; but then
I can afford to be — so that's not much.
As for success — if we must measure that
By the financial rule, 't is small, I grant you.
Yes, I have toiled, and lived laborious days,
And little can I show in evidence ;
And sometimes — sometimes, I am sick at heart,
And almost lose my faith in woman's power

To paint a rose, or even to mend a stocking,
As well as man can do. What would you have?"

" Now you speak reason. Let me see you act it!
Abandon this wild frenzy of the hour,
That would leave woman free to go all ways
A man may go! Why, look you, even in art,
Most epicene of all pursuits in life,
How man leaves woman always far behind!
Give up your foolish striving; and let Nature
And the world's order have their way with you."

" Small as the pittance is, yet I could earn
More, ten times, by my brush than by my needle."

" Ah! woman's sphere is that of the affections.
Ambition spoils her — spoils her as a woman.".

" Spoils her for whom?"
      " For man."

"Then woman's errand
Is not, like man's, self-culture, self-advancement,
But she must simply qualify herself
To be a mate for man : no obligation
Resting on man to qualify himself
To be a mate for woman ?"

"Ay, the man
Lives in the intellect ; the woman's life
Is that of the affections, the emotions ;
And her anatomy is proof of it."

"So have I often heard, but do not see.
Some women have I known, who could endure
Surgical scenes which many a strong man
Would faint at. We have had this dubious talk
Of woman's sphere far back as history goes :
'T is time now it were proved : let actions prove it ;
Let free experience, education prove it!
Why is it that the vilest drudgeries
Are put on woman, if her sphere be that

Of the affections only, the emotions?
He represents the intellect, and *she*
The affections only! Is it always so?
Let Malibran, or Mary Somerville,
De Staël, Browning, Stanton, Stowe, Bonheur,
Stand forth as proof of that cool platitude.
Use other arguments, if me you'd move.
Besides, I see not that your system makes
Any provision for that numerous class
To whom the affections are an Eden closed, —
The women who are single and compelled
To drudge for a precarious livelihood!
What of *their* sphere? What of the sphere of those
Who do not, by the sewing of a shirt,
Earn a meal's cost? Go tell them, when they venture
On an employment social custom makes
Peculiarly a man's, — that they become
Unwomanly! Go make them smile at that, —
Smile if they've not forgotten how to smile."

"I see that you're befogged, my little woman,
Chasing this ignis fatuus of the day!
Leave it, and settle down as woman should.
What has been always, must be to the end.
Always has woman been subordinate
In mind, in body, and in power, to man.
Let rhetoricians rave, and theorists
Spin their fine webs, — bow you to holy Nature,
And plant your feet upon the eternal fact."

"The little lifetime of the human race
You call — eternity! The other day
One of these old eternal wrongs was ended
Rather abruptly; yet good people thought
'T was impious to doubt it was eternal.
Because abuses have existed always,
May we not prove they are abuses still?
If for antiquity you plead, why not
Tell us the harem is the rule of nature,
The one solution of the woman problem?"

" Does not St. Paul — "

      " Excuse me. Beg no questions.
St. Paul to you may be infallible,
But Science is so unaccommodating,
If not irreverent, she'll not accept
His ipse dixit as an axiom.
Here, in our civilized society,
Is an increasing host of single women
Who do not find the means of livelihood
In the employments you call feminine.
What shall be done? And my reply is this:
Let every honest calling be as proper
For woman as for man; throw open all
Varieties of labor, skilled or rough,
To woman's choice and woman's competition.
Let *her* decide the question of the fitness.
Let her rake hay, or pitch it, if she'd rather
Do that than scrub a floor or wash and iron.
And, above all, let her equality
Be barred not at the ballot-box; endow her

With all the rights a citizen can claim;
Give her the suffrage; let her have — by right
And not by courtesy — a voice in shaping
The laws and institutions of the land.
And then, if after centuries of trial,
All shall turn out a fallacy, a failure,
The social scheme will readjust itself
On the old basis, and the world shall be
The wiser for the great experiment."

"But is sex nothing? Shall we recognize
No bounds that Nature clearly has defined,
Saying, with no uncertain tone, to one,
Do this, and to the other, Do thou that?
The rearing of young children and the care
Of households, — can we doubt where these belong?
Woman is but the complement of man
And not a monstrous contrariety.
Co-worker she, but no competitor!"

"All true, and no one doubts it! But why doubt
That perfect freedom is the best condition
For bringing out all that is best in woman
As well as man? Free culture, free occasion,
Higher responsibility, will make
A higher type of femininity,
Ay, of maternal femininity, —
Not derogate from that which now we have,
And which, through laws and limitations old,
Is artificial, morbid, and distort,
Except where Nature works in spite of all.
'Woman is but the complement of man!'
Granted. But why stop there? And why not add,
Man, too, is but the complement of woman?
And both are free! And Nature never meant,
For either, harder rule than that of Love,
Intelligent, and willing as the sun."

"Ah! were men angels, women something more,
Your plan might work; but now, in married life,

One must be absolute ; and who can doubt
That Nature points unerringly to man?"

"Then Nature's pointing is not always heeded.
Marriage should be a partnership of equals:
But now the theory would seem to be,
Man's laws must keep the weaker sex in order!
Man must do all the thinking, even for woman!
I don't believe it ; woman, too, can think,
Give her the training and the means of knowledge.
'O no!' cries man, 'the household and the child
Must claim her energies ; and all her training
Must be to qualify the wife and mother :
For one force loses when another gains,
Since Nature is a very strict accountant ;
And what you give the thinker or the artist,
You borrow from the mother and the wife.'
With equal truth, why not object to man

That what he gives the judge or politician
He borrows from the husband and the father?
The wife and mother best are qualified
When you allow the woman breadth of culture,
Give her an interest in all that makes
The human being's welfare, and a voice
In laws affecting her for good or ill.
To 'suckle fools and chronicle small beer'
Is not the whole intent of womanhood.
Even of maternity 't is not the height
To produce many children, but to have
Such as may be a blessing to their kind.
Let it be woman's pure prerogative,
Free and unswayed by man's imperious pleasure
(Which now too often is her only law),
To rule herself by her own highest instincts,
As her own sense of duty may approve, —
Holding that law for her as paramount
Which may best harmonize her whole of nature,
Educe her individuality,

Not by evading or profaning Nature,
But by a self-development entire."

"Enough, enough! Let us split hairs no longer!
You hold a crumpled letter in your hand;
You know the writer; you esteem, respect him;
And you 've had time to question your own heart.
What does it say? You blush, — you hesitate, —
That 's a good symptom. Now just hear me out:
If culture is your aim, how opportune
A chance is this! Affluence, leisure, study!
Would you help others? He will help you do it.
Is health an object? Soon, exempt from care,
Or cheered by travel, shall you see restored
Your early bloom and freshness. Would you find
In love a new and higher life? You start!
Now what 's the matter? Do not be a fool, —
A sentimentalist, forever groping
After the unattainable, the cloudy.
Come, be a little practical; consider

Your present state: look on that row of nails
Recipient of your wardrobe; see that bonnet,
All out of fashion by at least a month;
That rusty water-proof you call a cloak;
Those boots with the uneven heels; that pair
Of woollen gloves; this whole absurd array,
Where watchful Neatness battles Poverty,
But does not win the victory. Look there!
Would not a house on the great avenue
Be better than these beggarly surroundings?
Since you 're heart-free, why not at once say
  Yes?"

"Sweet fluent tempter, there you hit the mark!
Heart-free am I, and 't is because of that
You 're not entirely irresistible.
Your plea is simply that which lends excuse
To the poor cyprian whom we pass in scorn.
I 've done my utmost to persuade myself
That I might love this man,—in time might love:

But all my arguments, enforced by yours,
Do not persuade me.   I must give it up!"

Never was No administered more gently
Or more decisively than in her answer
To the proposal in the crumpled letter.

———

Musing before a picture Linda sat.
"In my poor little range of art," thought she,
"I feel an expert's confidence ; I know
These things are unexcelled ; and yet why is it
They do not bring their value?   Come, I'll try
Something more difficult, — put all my skill,
Knowledge, and work into one little piece."
Bravely she strove : it was a simple scene,
But with accessories as yet untried,
And done in oil with microscopic care ;
An open window with a distant landscape,
And on the window-sill a vase of flowers.

It was a triumph, and she knew it was.
"Come, little housekeeper," she said to Rachel,
"We'll go and seek our fortune." So she put
Under her arm the picture, and they went
To show it to the dealer who had bought
Most of her works. But on her way she met
A clerk of the establishment, who said:
"Come into Taylor's here and take an ice;
I'd like to tell you something for your good."

When they all three were seated, Brown began:
"You may not see me at the store again;
For a ship's cousin wants my place, and so,
With little ceremony, I'm dismissed.
Now, if you've no objection, tell me what
The old man gave you for that composition
In which a bird — a humming-bird, I think —
Follows a child who has a bunch of flowers."
"Yes, I remember. Well, 't was fifteen dollars."
"Whew! He said fifty. Is it possible?

You 've seen the chromo copy, I suppose?"
"The chromo? I 've seen nothing of a chromo.
Never has my consent been given to publish!"
"That 's little to the purpose, it would seem.
A hundred thousand copies have been sold
Of all your pieces, first and last. You stare?"
A light broke in on Linda. All at once
The mystery that hung upon her strivings
Lay solved; the cloud was lifted; and she saw
That all this while she had not weighed her tal-
    ents
In a false balance; had not been the dupe
Of her own aspirations and desires.
With eyes elate and hope up-springing fresh
In her glad heart, she cried, "And are you sure?"
"'T is easily confirmed. Go ask the printer;
Only my number is below the mark."

From Brown, then, Linda got particulars,
Showing 't was not a random utterance.

"'T is strange," she said, "that I 've not seen the chromos
At the shop windows." — "Only recently,"
Said he, "have they been sold here in the city;
The market has been chiefly at the West.
The old man thought it policy, perhaps,
To do it on the sly, lest you should know.
Well, well, in that bald head of his he has
A mine!" Then Linda struck the bell, and said:
"This is my entertainment, Mr. Brown;
Please let me pay for it." And Brown's "O no"
Was not so wholly irresistible
That Linda did not have her way in this.
They parted.

"Why, Miss Percival," said Rachel,
"You look precisely as you did that day
You fired the pistol in the woods, — you do!
I watched your eye, and knew you would not fail."
"'T is to bring down a different sort of game,
We now go forth." — "But you forget your pistol."

"This time we shall not need one. Did I not
Say we were going forth to seek our fortune?
Well, Rachel, my dear child, we've found it, —
    found it."
"O, I'm so glad! (How rapidly you walk!)
And shall we have the old piano back?"
"Ay, that we shall! And you shall go to-morrow
And take a present to the poor blind aunt
And her old mother, — for they love you well."
"A present! Why, Miss Percival, there's noth-
    ing
I do so love to do as to make presents.
I've made three in my lifetime; one a ring
Of tortoise-shell; and one — "
                        But here they entered
A picture-store. A man who stood alert,
With thumbs hooked in the arm-holes of his vest,
Advanced to welcome her. The "old man" he,
Of Brown's narration; not so very old,
However; not quite thirty-five, in fact.

The capital which made his note so good
Was a bald head ; a head you could not question ;
A head which was a pledge of solvency,
A warrant of respectability !
The scalp all glossy ; tufts above the ears !
This head he cultivated carefully,
And always took his hat off when he went
To ask a discount or to clinch a bargain.
" Ah ! my young friend, Miss Percival," he cried,
"You 've something choice there, if I 'm not mis-
    taken."
Linda took off the wrapper from her picture
And showed it.
              An expression of surprise
Came to the " old man's " features ; but he hid it
By making of his hand a cylinder
And looking through it, like a connoisseur.
These were his exclamations : " Clever ! Ay !
Style somewhat new ; landscape a shade too
    bright ;

The sky too blue, eh? Still a clever picture, —
One of your best. Shall we say twenty dollars?"
Taking the picture, Linda said, "Good morning!
I'm in a hurry now, and you'll excuse me."
"Will you not leave it?" — "No, I'm not dis-
    posed
To part with it at present." — "Thirty dollars
Would be a high price for it, but to aid you
I'll call it thirty." — "Could you not say fifty?"
"You're joking with me now, Miss Percival."
"Then we will end our pleasantry. Good by."
"Stay! You want money: I shall be ashamed
To let my partners know it, but to show
How far I'll go for your encouragement —
Come! I'll say fifty dollars."
                                    The "old man"
Lowered his head, so that the burnished scalp
Might strike her eye direct. Impenetrable
To that appeal, Linda said: "I can get
A hundred for it, I believe. Good day!"

"Stop, stop! For some time our intent has been
To make you a small present as a proof
Of our regard; now will I merge it in
A hundred dollars for the picture. Well?"
"Nay, I would rather not accept a favor.
I must go now,— will call again some day."
Desperate the "old man" moved his head about
In the most striking lights, and patted it
Wildly at last, as if by that mute act
To stay the unrelenting fugitive.
In vain! She glided off, and Rachel with her.
"Where now, Miss Percival?"— "To make a call
Upon a lawyer for advice, my dear."

Thoughtfully Diggin listened to the case,
So clearly stated that no part of it
Was left to disentangle. "Let me look,"
He said, "at your new picture; our first step
Shall be to fix the right of publication

In you alone. Expect from me no praise, —
For I'm no judge of art. Fine points of law,
Not fine points in a picture, have engaged
My thoughts these twenty years. While you wait
    here,
I'll send my clerk to copyright this painting.
What shall we call it?" — " Call it, if you please,
'The Prospect of the Flowers.'" — " That will do.
Entered according to — et cetera.
Your name is—" "Linda Percival."—"I thought
    so.
Here, Edward, go and take a copyright
Out for this work, 'The Prospect of the Flowers.'
First have it photographed, and then deposit
The photographic copy with the Court."

Then Diggin paced the room awhile, and ran
Through his lank hair his fingers nervously.
At length his plan took shape; he stopped and
    said

"You shall take back your picture to this dealer;
Tell him 't is not for sale, but get his promise
To have it, for a fortnight, well displayed
At his shop window. This he 'll not refuse.
Don't sell at any price. What 's your address?
Edward shall go with you : 't is well to have
A witness at this juncture. Write me down
The printer's name Brown gave you. Ay, that 's
    right.
Now go; and if the picture is removed —
For purposes we 'll not anticipate —
As it will be — we 'll corner the 'old man,'
And his bald head sha' n't save him. By the way,
If you want money let me be your banker;
I 'm well content to risk a thousand dollars
On the result of my experiment."

The picture was removed, as he foretold.
Ten weeks went by; then Linda got it back.
"It is the pleasant season," said the lawyer;

"Here are three hundred dollars. You start
    back!
Miss Linda, I shall charge you ten per cent
On all you borrow. Oh! You do not like
To be in debt. This is my risk, not yours.
If I recover nothing, then no debt
Shall be by you incurred, — so runs the bond!
Truly, now, 't is no sentimental loan:
I trust another's solvency, not yours.
At length you understand me, — you consent!
Now do not go to work; but you and Rachel
Go spend a long vacation at the seaside.
You want repose and sunshine and pure air.
Be in no hurry to return. The longer
You 're gone, the better. For a year at least
We must keep dark. That puzzles you. No
    matter.
Here, take my card, and should you any time
Need money, do not hesitate to draw
On me for funds. There! Not a word! Good
    by!"

In the cars, eastward bound! A clear, bright day
After a rain-storm; and, on both sides, verdure;
Trees waving salutations, waters gleaming.
The brightness had its type in Linda's looks,
As, with her little protégée, she sat
And savored all the beauty, all the bloom.
On the seat back of them, two gentlemen
Chatted at intervals in tones which Linda
Could hardly fail to hear, though little heeding.
But now and then, almost unconsciously,
She found herself attending to their prattle.
Said Gossip Number One: " You see that veteran
In the straw hat, and the young man beside him:
Father and son are they. Old Lothian,
Five months ago, was high among the trusted
Of our chief bankers; Charles, his only son,
By a maternal uncle's death enriched,
Kept out of Wall Street; turned a stolid ear
To all high-mounting schemes for doubling wealth,
His taste inclining him to art and letters.

But Lothian had a partner, Judd, — a scamp,
As the result made evident ; and Judd
One day was missing ; bonds, securities,
And bills, deposits of confiding folk,
Guardians, and widows, and old men retired,
All had been gobbled up by Judd — converted
Into hard cash — and Judd had disappeared.
Despair for Lothian ! a man whose word
No legal form could make more absolute.
Crushed, mortified, and rendered powerless,
He could not breast the storm. The mental
       strain
Threw him upon his bed, and there he lay
Till Charles, from Italy in haste returning,
Found his old sire emaciate and half dead
From wounded honor. 'Come ! no more of this !'
Cried Charles ; 'how happened it that you forgot
You had a son ? All shall be well, my father.'
He paid off all the liabilities,
And found himself without three thousand dollars

Out of a fortune of at least a million.
What shall we call him, imbecile or saint?
His plan is now to set up as a teacher.
Of such a teacher let each thrifty father
Beware, or he may see his only son
Turn out a poor enthusiast, — perhaps —
Who knows? — an advocate of woman's rights!"

Attracted by the story, Linda tried
To get a sight of him, the simpleton;
And, when she saw his face, it seemed to her
Strangely familiar. Was it in a dream
That she had once beheld it? Vain the attempt
Of peering memory to fix the where
And when of the encounter! Yet she knew
That with it was allied a grateful thought.
Then Rachel spoke and made the puzzle clear:
"The man who sent us in his carriage home,
That day you fainted, — don't you recollect?"
"Ay, surely! 't is the same. No dream-face that!

Charles Lothian, is he ? If his acts are folly,
Then may I be a fool ! Such fools are rare.
How tender of his father he appears !
I wonder where they 're going."

        When, at Springfield,
Father and son got out, a sigh, or rather
The ghost of one, and hardly audible,
Escaped from Linda. Then Charles Lothian,
While the cars waited, caught her eye, and bowed.
So he remembered her ! " Now that was odd.
But the bell sounds ; the locomotive puffs ;
The train moves on. Charles Lothian, good by !
Eastward we go ; away from you — away —
Never to meet again in this wide world ; —
Like ships that in mid-ocean meet and part,
To meet no more — O, nevermore — perchance ! "

VI.

BY THE SEASIDE.

BORNE swiftly to the North Cape of the Bay,
  Still on the wings of steam the travellers went;
And tenderly the purple sunset smiled
Upon their journey's end; a little cottage
With oaks and pines behind it, and, before,
High ocean crags, and under them the ocean,
Unintercepted far as sight could reach!
Foliage and waves! A combination rare

Of lofty sylvan table-land, and then —
No barren strip to mar the interval —
The watery waste, the ever-changing main!
Old Ocean, with a diadem of verdure
Crowning the summit where his reach was stayed!
The shore, a line of rocks precipitous,
Piled on each other, leaving chasms profound,
Into whose rifts the foamy waters rushed
With gurgling roar, then flowed in runlets back
Till the surge drove them furiously in,
Shaking with thunderous bass the cloven granite!
Yet to the earth-line of the tumbled cliffs
The wild grass crept; the sweet-leafed bayberry
Scented the briny air; the fern, the sumach,
The prostrate juniper, the flowering thorn,
The blueberry, the clinging blackberry,
Tangled the fragrant sod; and in their midst
The red rose bloomed, wet with the drifted spray.

From the main shore cut off, and isolated
By the invading, the circumfluent waves,
A rock which time had made an island, spread
With a small patch of brine-defying herbage,
Is known as Norman's Woe ; for, on this rock,
Two hundred years ago, was Captain Norman,
In his good ship from England, driven and
    wrecked
In a wild storm, and every life was lost.

Stand on the cliff near by, — southeasterly
Are only waves on waves to the horizon ;
But easterly, less than two miles across,
And forming with the coast-line, whence you
    look,
The harbor's entrance, stretches Eastern Point,
A lighthouse at its end ; a mile of land
Arm-like thrust out to keep the ocean off;
So narrow that beyond its width, due east,
You see the Atlantic glittering, hardly made
Less inconspicuous by the intervention.

The cottage fare, the renovating breeze,
The grove, the piny odors, and the flowers,
Rambles at morning and the twilight time,
Sea-bathing, joyous and exhilarant,
Siestas on the rocks, with inhalations
Of the pure breathings of the ocean-tide, —
Soon wrought in both the maidens visible change.
Each day their walks grew longer, till at last
A ten-mile tramp was no infrequent one.

"And where to-day?" asked Rachel, one fair morning.
"To Eastern Point," said Linda; "with our baskets!
For berries, there's no place like Eastern Point;
Blackberries, whortleberries, pigeon-pears, —
All we shall find in prodigality!"
And so by what was once the old stage-road
Contiguous to the shore, and through the woods, —

Though long abandoned save by scenery-hunters,
And overgrown with grass and vines and bushes;
Then leaving on their right the wooded hill
Named from the rattlesnakes, now obsolete;
Then by the Cove, and by the bend of shore
Over Stage-rocks, by little Half-moon beach,
Across the Cut, the Creek, by the Hotel,
And through the village, even to Eastern Point, —
The maidens went, and had a happy day.
And, when the setting sun blazed clear and mild,
And every little cloud was steeped in crimson,
To a small wharf upon the harbor side,
Along the beach they strolled, and looked across
The stretch of wave to Norman's Woe; — and Linda
Wistfully said: "Heigho! I own I'm tired;
And you, too, Rachel, you look travel-worn,
And hardly good for four miles more of road.
Could we but make this short cut over water!

What would I give now for a boat to take us
To Webber's Cove! O, if some timely oarsman
Would only come and say, 'Fair demoiselles,
My skiff lies yonder, rocking on the tide,
And eager to convey you to your home!'
Then would I —— Rachel!"

        "What, Miss Percival?"
"Look at those men descending from the ridge!"
"Well, I can see an old man and a young."
"And is that all you have to say of them?"
"How should I know about them? Ah! I see!
Those are the two we met three weeks ago, —
The day we left New York, — met in the cars."
"Ay, Rachel, and their name is Lothian;
Father and son are they. Who would have
  thought
That they would find their way to Eastern
  Point?"
"Why not, as well as we, Miss Percival?
Look! To the wharf they go; and there, beside
  it,

If I 'm not much mistaken, lies a boat.
The wished-for oarsman he ! O, this is luck !
They 're going to the boat, — he 'll row us over,
I 'll run and ask him. See you to my basket."
" Rachel ! Stop, Rachel ! Fie, you forward girl !
Don't think of it: come back ! back, back, I
    say ! "

But Rachel did not hear, or would not heed,
Straight to the boat she ran, and, as the men
Drew nigh and stopped, — to Linda's dire dismay
She went up and accosted them, and pointed
To Norman's Woe, — then back to her com-
    panion, —
And then, with gesture eloquent of thanks
For some reply the younger man had made,
She seemed to lead the way, and he to follow
Along the foot-path to the granite bench
Where Linda sat, abashed and wondering.
And, when they stood before her, Rachel said

"Miss Percival, here's Mr. Lothian;
He has a boat near by, and will be glad
To give us seats and row us both across."
Charles Lothian bowed, and Linda, blushing,
  said,
"Against my orders did this little lady
Accost you, sir, but I will not affect
Regret at her success, if you're content."
"More than content, I'm very glad," said Charles;
"My boat is amply large enough for four,
And we are bound, it seems, all the same way.
My father and myself have taken rooms
At Mistress Moore's, not far from where you live:
So count your obligation very slight."
"An obligation not the first!" said Linda.
"So much the better!" said Charles Lothian:
"Come, take my arm, and let me hold your
  basket.
What noble blackberries! I'll taste of one."
"Why not of two? As many as you will?"

"Thank you. You've been adventurous, it
 seems."
"Yes, Fortune favors the adventurous:
See the old proverb verified to-day!"
"Praise a good day when ended. Here's my
 father:
Father, Miss Percival!" The senior bowed,
And said, "I used to know —" And then, as if
Checked by a reminiscence that might be
Unwelcome, he was silent, and they went
All to the boat. "Please let me take an oar,"
Said Linda. "Can you row?" asked Charles.
 "A little!
My father taught me." Then old Lothian
Looked at her with a scrutinizing glance.

The ocean billows melted into one,
And that stretched level as a marble floor.
All winds were hushed, and only sunset tints
From purple cloudlets, edged with fiery gold,

And a bright crimson fleece the sun had left,
Fell on the liquid plain incarnadined.
The very pulse of ocean now was mute;
From the far-off profound, no throb, no swell!
Motionless on the coastwise ships the sails
Hung limp and white, their very shadows white.
The lighthouse windows drank the kindling red,
And flashed and gleamed as if the lamps were lit.

"A heavenly eve!" sighed Linda, rapt in praise,
As with poised oars the two looked oceanward.
Then, keeping time, they pulled out from the shore.
"But you row well!" cried Charles. "I might return
The compliment," said Linda. "See that duck!
How near, how still he floats! He seems to know
The holy time will keep him safe from harm."
"Had I a gun," said Charles — "You would not use it,"

Cried Linda, flushing. "And why not?" quoth
    he.
"'Nobility obliges'; sympathy
Now makes all nature one and intimate;
And we'd respect, even in a duck, his share
In this tranquillity, this perfect rest."
"I'm glad, then, that I'm gunless," Charles re-
    plied.
"Hear him!" the sire exclaimed; "he'd have you
    think
He's a great sportsman. Be not duped, my
    dear!
He will not shoot nor fish! He got a wound
At Gettysburg, I grant you, — what of that?
He would far rather face a battery
Than kill a duck, or even hook a cunner."
"See now," said Charles, "the mischievous effect
Of this exhilarating Cape Ann air!
'T is the first taunt I've heard from lips of his
Since my return from Europe. Look you,
    father,

If I'm to be exposed before young ladies,
Your rations shall be stopped, and your supply
Of oxygen reduced, — with no more joking.
Don't eye those berries so feloniously.
Because you've now an appetite, — because
You've just begun to gain a little flesh, —
Must I be made the target of your jeers?"

Smiling, but with sad eyes, the father said:
"Ah! Charlie, Charlie, when I think of it, —
Think how you've thrown, poor boy, your very
    life
Into the breach of ruin made for me, —
Sacrificed all, to draw the lethal dart
Out of my wounded honor — to restore — "
"Give us a song, Miss Percival, a song!"
Charles, interrupting, said. "The time, the place,
Call for a song. Look! All the lighthouses
Flash greeting to the night. There Eastern
    Point

Flames out! Lo, little Ten Pound Island follows!
See Baker's Island kindling! Marblehead '
Ablaze! Egg Rock, too, off Nahant, on fire!
And Boston Light winking at Minot's Ledge!
Like the wise virgins, all, with ready lamps!
Now might I turn fire-worshipper, and bow
In adoration at this solemn rite :
I 'll compromise, however, for a song."
"Lest you turn Pagan, then, I 'll sing," quoth
      Linda.
And, while they rested on their oars, she sang.

LINDA'S SONG.

   A little bird flew
     To the top of a tree :
  The sky it was blue,
     And the bird sang to me.
So tender and true was the strain
The singer, I hoped, would remain :
O little bird, stay and prolong
The rapture the grief of that song!

A little thought came,
    Came out of my heart;
It whispered a name
    That made me to start:
And the rose-colored breath of my sigh
Flushed the earth and the sea and the sky.
Delay, little thought! O, delay,
And gladden my life with thy ray!

"Such singing lured Ulysses to the rocks!"
Old Lothian said, applauding. "Charles, look out,
Or, ere we reck of it, this reckless siren
Will have us all a wreck on Norman's Woe.
See to your oars! Where are we drifting, man?"
"Who would not drift on such a night as this?"
Said Charles; "all's right." Then, heading for
    the Cove,
Slowly and steadily the rowers pulled.

But, when the moon shone crescent in the west,
And the faint outline of the part obscured
Thread-like curved visible from horn to horn, —

And Jupiter, supreme among the orbs,
And Mars, with rutilating beam, came forth,
And the great concave opened like a flower,
Unfolding firmaments and galaxies,
Sparkling with separate stars, or snowy white
With undistinguishable suns beyond, —
They paused and rested on their oars again,
And looked around, — in adoration looked.
For, gazing on the inconceivable,
They felt God is, though inconceivable ; —
And, while they mutely worshipped, suddenly
A change came over Linda's countenance,
And her glazed mortal eyes were functionless ;
For there, before her in the boat, stood two
Unbidden, not unwelcome passengers,
Her father and her mother. . . . .
       " Why, Miss Linda,
Wake! Are you sleeping ? What has been the
  matter ?
Here we 've been waiting for you full five minutes.

And I have called, and Mr. Lothian
He too has called, and yet you make no answer!"
"Rachel! What is it? There! Excuse me all,
If I seemed impolite. Now, then, I'm ready.
A strong pull shall it be? So! Let her dart!"

And in ten minutes they were at the landing
And on their homeward way; and, as they parted,
The spoils were shared, and the old man accepted
One of the baskets, and all cried, "Good night!"

The morning sea-fog like an incense rose
Up to the sun and perished in his beam;
The sky's blue promise brightened through the
  veil.
With her unopened sketch-book in her hand,
Linda stood on the summit looking down
On Norman's Woe, and felt upon her brow
The cooling haze that foiled the August heat.

Near her knelt Rachel, hunting curiously
For the fine purple algæ of the clefts.
Good cause had Linda for a cheerful heart;
For had she not that day received by mail
A copy of " The Prospect of the Flowers," —
Published in chromo, and these words from
     Diggin?
"Your future is assured: my bait is swallowed,
Bait, hook, and sinker, all; now let our fish
Have line enough and time enough for play,
And we will land him safely by and by.
A good fat fish he is, and thinks he's cunning.
Enclosed you'll find a hundred-dollar bill;
Please send me a receipt.   Keep very quiet."

Yet Linda was not altogether happy.
Why was it that Charles Lothian had called
Once, and once only, after their adventure?
Called just to ask her, How she found herself?
And, Did she overtask herself in rowing?

How happened it, in all her walks and rambles,
They rarely met, or, if they met, a bow
Formal and cold was all the interview?
While thus she mused, she started at a cry:
"Ah! here's our siren, cumbent on the rocks!
Where should a siren be, if not on rocks?"
Old Lothian's voice! He came with rod and line
To try an angler's luck. Behind him stepped
Charles, who stood still, as if arrested, when
He noticed Linda.
                Then, as if relenting
In some resolve, he jumped from rock to rock
To where she leaned; and, greeting her, inquired:
"Have you been sketching?" — "No, for indo-
    lence
Is now my occupation." — "Here's a book;
May I not look at it?" — "You may." — "Is this
An album?" — "'T is my sketch-book." — "Do
    you mean
These are your sketches, and original?"

"Ay, truly, mine; from nature every one."
"But here we have high art! No amateur
Could color flower like that."—"Ah! there you
  touch me;
For I'm no amateur in painting flowers,—
I get my living by it."—"I could praise
That sea-view also,—what a depth of sky!
That beach,—that schooner flying from a squall,—
If I'm a judge, here's something more than skill!"

Then the discourse slid off to woman's rights;
For Lothian held a newspaper which told
Of some convention, the report of which
Might raise a smile. One of the lady speakers,
It seems, would give her sex the privilege
Of taking the initiative in wooing,
If so disposed!
    "Indeed, why not?" cried Linda.
"Indeed, you almost take my breath away
With your Why not, Miss Percival! Why not?"

"Yes, I repeat, — if so disposed, why not?
For why should woman any more than man
Play the dissembler, with so much at stake?
I know the ready taunt that here will rise:
'Already none too backward are our girls
In husband-seeking.' Seeking in what way?
Seeking by stratagem and management, —
Not by frank, honest means! What food for mirth
'T would give to shallow men to see a woman
Court the relation, intertwined with all
Of purest happiness that she may crave, —
The ties of wife and mother! O, what pointing,
Sneering, and joking! And yet why should care
Thoughtful and pure and wisely provident,
That Nature's sacred prompting shall not fail,
Be one thing for a man, and quite another
For her, the woman?' Why this flimsy mask?
This playing of a part, put on to suit,
Not the heart's need, but Fashion custom-bound?
Feigning we must be sought, and never seek?

Now, through these social hindrances and bars,
The bold, perhaps the intriguing, carry off
Prizes the true and modest ought to win.
And so we hear it coarsely said of husbands,
' Better a poor one far, than none at all ! '
A thought ignoble, and which no true woman
Should harbor for a moment. Give her freedom,
Freedom to seek, and she 'll not harbor it !
Because if woman, equally with man,
Were privileged thus, she would discriminate
Much more than now, and fewer sordid unions
Would be the sure result. For what if man
Were chained to singleness until some woman
Might seek his hand in marriage, would he be
Likely as now to make a wise election ?
Would he not say, ' Time flies ; my chances lessen
And I must plainly take what I can get ? '
True, there are mercenary men enough,
Seeking rich dowries ; they 'd find fewer dupes,
Were women free as men to seek and choose,

Banish the senseless inequality,
And you make marriage less a vulgar game
In which one tries to circumvent the other.
Oh! all this morbid ribaldry of *men*,
And all this passive imbecility,
And superstitious inactivity,
Dissimulation and improvidence,
False shame and lazy prejudice of *women*,
Where the great miracle of sex concerns us,
And Candor should be innocently wise,
And Knowledge should be reverently free, —
Is against nature, — helps to hide the way
Out of the social horrors that confound us,
And launches thousands into paths impure,
Shutting them out from holy parentage."

"I hold," said Charles, "the question is not one
Of reasoning, but of simple sentiment.
As it would shock me, should a woman speak
In virile baritone, so would I shudder

To hear a grave proposal marriageward
In alto or soprano."
     "'T would depend!
Depend on love," said Linda; "love potential,
Or present." — "Nay, 't would frighten love!"
  cried Charles, —
"Kill it outright." — "Then would it not be love!
What! would you love a woman less because
She durst avow her love, before the cue
Had been imparted by your lordly lips?
Rare love would that be truly which could freeze
Because the truth came candid from her heart,
And in advance of the proprieties!"
"But may the woman I could love," cried
  Charles,
"Forbear at least the rash experiment!"
"I doubt," said Linda, "if you know your heart;
For hearts look to the substance, not the form.
Why should not woman seek her happiness
With brow as unabashed as man may wear

In seeking his? Ah! lack of candor here
Works more regrets, for woman and for man,
Than we can reckon. Let but woman feel
That in the social scheme she's not a cipher,
The remedy, be sure, is not far off."

"To me it seems," said Lothian, "that you war
Against our natural instincts: have they not
Settled the point, even as the world has done?"
Said Linda: "Instincts differ; they may be
Results of shallow prejudice or custom.
The Turk will tell you that polygamy
Is instinct; and the savage who stalks on
In dirty painted grandeur, while his squaw
Carries the burdens, might reply that instinct
Regulates that. So instinct proves too much.
Queens and great heiresses are privileged
To intimate their matrimonial choice, —
Simply because superiority
In power or riches gives an apt excuse:

Let a plurality of women have
The wealth and power, and you might see reversed
What now you call an instinct. When a higher
Civilization shall make woman less
Dependent for protection and support
On man's caprice or pleasure, there may be
A higher sort of woman; one who shall
Feel that her lot is more in her own hands,
And she, like man, a free controlling force,
Not a mere pensioner on paternal bounty
Until some sultan throws the handkerchief."

A cry of triumph from the fisherman,
Exuberant at having caught a bass,
Here ended the discussion, leaving Linda
With the last word. Charles went to chat with
    Rachel;
And Linda, summoned by vociferations
From the excited, the transported captor,
Descended to inspect the amazing fish.

"A beauty, is it not, Miss Percival?
A rare one, too, for this part of the coast!
'T will be a study how to have it cooked.
Now sit here, in the shadow of this rock.
Your father's name was Albert Percival?
So I supposed. I 've often heard my wife
Speak of him as of one she knew was wronged
Most foully in his wrestle with the law.
Have you not met with Harriet Percival?"
"Once only, and our interview was brief.
Is she not married?" — "No, nor like to be,
Although her fortune is a pretty one,
Even for these times, — two millions, I believe;
All which her mother may inherit soon;
For Harriet is an invalid, but hoards
Her income quite as thriftily as if
She looked for progeny and length of days.
The mother, as you may not be aware,
Has married an aspiring gentleman
Who means to build a palace on the Hudson,
And Harriet's money hence is greatly needed."

The mist now cleared, and the sun shone in
    power,
So that the heat soon drove them to the woods.
The senior took his capture home for dinner;
Rachel strolled, picking berries by the brook;
And, under lofty pines, sat Charles and Linda,
And talked discursively, till Linda's thoughts,
Inclining now to memory, now to hope,
Vibrating from the future to the past,
Took, in a silent mood, this rhythmic form.

UNDER THE PINES.

O pine-trees! bid the busy breeze be still
That through your tops roars like the constant surge:
Such was the sound I heard in happy days
    Under the pines.

In happy days, when those I loved were by;
In happy days, when love was daily food;
And jocund childhood, finding it, found joy
    Under the pines.

Again I hear the west-wind in your tops;
Again I scent the odor you exhale;
But sound and odor now provoke but tears
    Under the pines.

O pine-trees! shall a different joy be mine,
One day when I shall seek your fragrant shade?
Whisper it faintly, breezes, to my heart
    Under the pines

"Truly, Miss Percival, you puzzle me,"
Said Charles, upon her silent revery
Breaking abruptly in: "ay, you could fire
And wound the villain bearing off the child,
And you can brave the radical extreme
On this great woman question of the day, —
Yet do you seem a very woman still,
And not at all like any man I know, —
Not even like an undeveloped man!
And I'm not greatly exercised by fear,
Leaning here by your side thus lazily."
"Don't mock me now," said Linda; "I'm not
  armed;

Be generous, therefore, in your raillery."
"Not armed? Then will I venture to propose
That when the tide is low this afternoon
We try the beach on horseback. Will you ven-
    ture?"
The joy that sparkled in her eyes said "Yes"
Before her tongue could duplicate assent.
Said Charles, "I'll bring the horses round at six."
"I will be ready, Mr. Lothian."

There was no breach of punctuality:
Though sighs, from deeper founts than tears, were
    heaved,
When she drew forth the summer riding-habit
Worn last when in the saddle with her father.
"Here are the horses at the door!" cried Rachel;
"A bay horse and a black; the bay is yours."
When they were mounted, Lothian remarked:
"Little Good Harbor Beach shall be our point;
So called because an Indian once pronounced

The harbor 'little good,' meaning 'quite bad';
A broad and open beach, from which you see
Running out southerly the ocean side
Of Eastern Point; its lofty landward end
Gray with huge cliffs. There shall you mark
    'Bass Rock,'
Rare outlook when a storm-wind from the east
Hurls the Atlantic up the craggy heights."

The air was genial, and a rapid trot
Soon brought them to the beach. The ebb had
    left
A level stretch of sand, wide, smooth, and hard,
With not a hoof-mark on the glistening plain.
The horses tossed their heads with snorting
    pride,
Feeling the ocean breeze, as curved and fell
Up the long line the creeping fringe of foam,
Then backward slid in undulating glass,
While all the west in Tyrian splendor flamed.

"But this is life!" cried Linda, as she put
Her horse to all his speed, and shook her whip.
They skimmed the sand, they chased the flying
    wave,
They walked their horses slow along the beach :
And, as the light fell on a far-off sail,
And made it a white glory to the eye,
Said Linda : "See ! it fades into the gray,
And now 't is dim, and now is seen no more !
Yet would a little height reveal it still.
So fade from memory scenes which higher points
Of vision shall reveal : the beautiful,
The good, shall never die ; and so to-day
Shall be a lasting, everlasting joy !"

"Would I might see more of such days !" said he,
"In the obscure before me ! Fate forbids.
My time of idlesse terminates to-night.
To-morrow to the city we return.
Thither I go, to open, in October,

A private school; and I must find a house
And make my preparations."

                                      On they rode,
After these words, in silence for a mile
Upon their homeward way. Then Lothian:
"And what will your address be, in the city?"
"I do not know, nor care," said Linda, switching
Her horse's ear, to start a quicker trot.
Another mile of silence! "Look!" cried he;
"The lighthouse light salutes us!" — "Yes, I
     see."
"Why do you go so fast?" — "I'll slacken speed
If you desire it. There!" They breathed their
     horses;
Then Lothian: "Indeed, I hope that we
Shall meet again." — "Why not? The world is
     wide,
But I have known a letter in a bottle,
Flung over in mid-ocean, to be found
And reach its owner. Doubtless, we may meet."
"I'm glad to find you confident of that."

Silence again! And so they rode along
Till they saw Rachel coming from the house
To greet them. Charles helped Linda to dismount,
Held out his hand, and said, "Good by, Miss Linda."
"Good by!" she cheerily answered; "bid your father
Good by for me. And so you go indeed
To-morrow?" — "Yes, we may not meet again."
"Well; pleasant journey!" — "Thank you. Good by, Rachel."
He rode away, leading her panting horse;
And, when the trees concealed him, Linda rushed
Up stairs, and locked the door, and wept awhile.

As, early the next morning, she looked forth
On the blue ocean from the open window,
"Now, then, for work!" she cried, and drew her palm

Across her brow, as if to thrust away
Thoughts that too perseveringly came back
She heard a step. 'T is he! "I hardly hoped,
Miss Percival, to find you up so early:
Good by, once more!" — "Good by! Don't miss
    the train."
At this a shadow fell on Lothian's face,
As with uplifted hat and thwarted smile,
He turned away. Then off with hasty stride
He walked and struck the bushes listlessly.

"What did I mean by speaking so?" said Linda,
With hand outstretched, as if to draw him back.
"Poor fellow! He looked sad; but why — but
    why
Is he so undemonstrative? And why
Could he not ask again for my address,
I 'd like to know?" Poor Linda! She could
    preach,
But, like her elders, could not always practise.

VII.

FROM LINDA'S DIARY.

I.

HOME again! Home? what satire in the word!
If home is where the heart is, where's my home?
Well: here's my easel; here my old piano;
Here the memorials of my early days!
Here let me try at least to be content.
This din of rolling wheels beneath my window,
Let it renew for me the ocean's roar!

II.

It is the heart makes music musical!
My neighbor has a mocking-bird: its song
Has been as little heeded as the noise
Of rattling wheels incessant; but to-day
One of its strains brought all Elysium back
Into my heart. What was it? What the tie
Linking it with some inexpressive joy?
At length I solve the mystery! Those notes,
Pensively slow and sadly exquisite,
Were what the wood-thrush piped at early dawn
After that evening passage in the boat,
When stars came out, that never more shall set.
Oh! sweet and clear the measured cadence fell
Upon my ear in slumber — and I woke!
I woke, and listened while the first faint flush
Of day was in the east; while yet the grove
Showed only purple gloom, and on the beach
The tidal waves with intermittent rush

Broke lazily and lent their mingling chime.
And O the unreckoned riches of the soul!
The possible beatitudes, of which
A glimpse is given, a transitory glimpse,
So rarely in a lifetime! Then it was,
Hearing that strain, as if all joy the Past
Had in its keeping, — all the Future held, —
All love, all adoration, and all beauty, —
Made for a moment the soul's atmosphere,
And lifted it to bliss unspeakable.
O splendor fugitive! O transport rare!
Transfiguring and glorifying life!

III.

This strange, inexplicable human heart!
My lawyer sends me more good news; he writes:
" The picture's sale will reach ten thousand copies,
And for the first year only! We shall have
A big bill to send in; and do not fear
But the 'old man' will pay it, every dime.

To escape the heavy damages the law
Allows for such infringement, he'll be glad
To compromise for the amount I fix;
And what I shall compel him to disgorge
Will simply be fair copyright on all
Your published works; and this will give you clear
Some fifteen thousand dollars, not to speak
Of a fixed interest in future sales."
So writes my lawyer. Now one would suppose
That news like this would make me light of heart,
Spur my ambition; and, as taste of blood
Fires the pet tiger, even so touch of gold
Would rouse the sacred appetite of gain.
But with attainment cometh apathy;
And I was somewhat happier, methinks,
When life was all a struggle, and the prayer,
"Give me my daily bread," had anxious meaning.

IV.

Is it then true that woman's proper sphere
Is in the affections? that she's out of place
When these are balked, and science, art, or trade
Has won the dedication of her thought?
Nay! the affections are for all; and he,
Or she, has most of life, who has them most.
O, not an attribute of sex are they!
Heart loneliness is loneliness indeed,
But not for woman any more than man,
Were she so trained, her active faculties
Could have a worthy aim.
                              What worthier,
Than the pursuit, the discipline of beauty?
He who finds beauty helps to interpret God:
For not an irreligious heart can dwell
In him who sees and knows the beautiful.
I'll not believe that one whom Art has chosen
For a high priest can be irreverent,
Sordid, unloving; his veil-piercing eye

Sees not in life the beauty till it sees
God and the life beyond; not in a dream
Of Pantheistic revery where all
In all is lost, diluted, and absorbed,
And consciousness and personality
Vanish like smoke forever; but all real,
Distinct, and individual, though all
Eternally dependent on the One!
Who gave the Eye to see, shall He not see?
Who gave the Heart to feel, shall He not love?
Of knowledge infinite we know a letter,
A syllable or two, and thirst for more:
Is there not One, Teacher at once and Cause,
Who comprehends all beauty and all science,
Holding infinity, that, step by step,
We may advance, and find, in what seems good
To Him, our gladness and our being's crown?
If this were not, then what a toy the world!
And what a mockery these suns and systems!
And how like pumping at an empty cistern
Were it to live and study and aspire!

Come, then, O Art! and warm me with thy smile!
Flash on my inward sight thy radiant shapes!
August interpreter of thoughts divine,
Whether in sound, or word, or form revealed!
Pledge and credential of immortal life!
Grand arbiter of truth! Consoler! come!
Come, help even me to seek thee and to find!

V.

Winter is here again; it sees me still
At work upon my picture. This presents
Two vases, filled with flowers, upon a slab.
"Which will you choose?" I call it: 't is in oil.
Three hours a day are all I give to it,
So fine the work, so trying to the eyes.
Thus have I ample time for teaching Rachel:
A good child and affectionate! I've found
Her aptitude; she has a taste in bonnets,
With an inventive skill in ornament.
And so I have her regularly taught

By an accomplished milliner; and Rachel
Already promises to lead her teacher.
Had I a fortune, still I 'd have her feel
That she must conquer something worthily;
Something to occupy her active powers,
And yield a fair support, should need require.

VI.

Whom should I meet to-day but Meredith!
My washerwoman, Ellen Blount, is ill,
So ill I fear she never will be well.
'T is the old story, every day renewed:
A little humble, tender-hearted woman,
Tied to a husband whom to call a brute
Would be to vilify the quadrupeds!
A fellow, who must have his pipe, his whiskey,
And his good dinner, let what may befall
His wife and children. He could take the pittance
She got from her hard toil, and spend it on
Himself and his companions of the jug.

When out of work, as he would often be,
Then double toil for her! with peevish words
From him, the sole requital of it all!
Child after child she bore him ; but, compelled
Too quickly after childbirth to return
To the old wash-tub, all her sufferings
Reacted on the children, and they died,
Haply in infancy the most of them, —
Until but one was left, — a little boy,
Puny and pale, gentle and uncomplaining,
With all the mother staring from his eyes
In hollow, anxious, pitiful appeal.
In this one relic all her love and hope
And all that made her life endurable
At length were centred. She had saved a dollar
To buy for him a pair of overshoes ;
But, as she went to get them, Blount waylaid her,
Learnt that she had the money, forced it from her.
Poor Teddy had to go without his shoes.
'T was when the January thaw had made

The streets a-reek with mud and melting snow.
Poor Teddy wet his feet, took cold, and died.
" Come soon, mamma," were his last feeble words.
Blount was a cunning ruffian ; well he knew
How far to go, and where and when to pause.
Fluent and specious with his tongue, he kept,
In his small sphere, a certain show of credit ;
And he could blow in tune for mother church,
Though few the pennies he himself would give her.
" Cast off the wretch," was my advice to Ellen.
She loved him not ; she might as well have tried
To love a load that galled and wearied her.
But custom, social fear, and, above all,
Those sacramental manacles the church
Had bound her in, and to the end would keep,
Forbade the poor, scared, helpless little woman
To free herself, by one condign resolve,
From the foul incubus that sucked her life.
So a false sense of duty kept her tied,
Feeding in him all that was pitiless.

And now she's dying. I had gone to-day
To take some little dainties, cream and fruit,
And there, administering consolation,
Was Meredith.
                    Hearing his tones of faith,
Seeing his saintly look of sympathy,
I felt, there being between us no dissent
In spirit, dogmas were of small account :
And so I knelt and listened to his prayer.
At length he noticed me, and recognized.
" Miss Percival ! " he cried ; " can this be you ?
But when and why did you return from England ? "
" I've never been in England, never been
Out of my native country," I replied.
" But that is unaccountable," said he ;
" For I've seen letters, written as from you,
Signed with your name, acknowledging receipts
Of certain sums of money, dated London."
" No money have I had but what I've earned,"
Was my reply ; " and who should send me money ? "

Said he: "I have a carriage at the door;
I would learn more of this; you'll not object
To take a seat with me? Thank you; that's
    right."

Leaving the patient in good hands, we went,
And through the noisy streets drove to the Park.
Then all I'd ever known about my parents
He drew from me; and all my history
Since I had parted from him; noted down
Carefully my address, and gave me his.
Then to my lodgings driving with me back,
He left me with a *Benedicite!*
He's rich: has he been sending money, then?
What means it all? Conjecture finds no clew.

VII.

Gently as thistle-downs are borne away
From the dry stem, went Ellen yesterday.
I heard her dying utterance; it was:

"I'm coming, Teddy! Bless you, dear Miss Linda!"
No priest was by, so sudden was her going.
When Blount came in, there was no tenderness
In his sleek, gluttonous look; although he tried,
Behind his handkerchief, to play the mourner.
What will he do without a drudge to tread on?
Counting himself a privileged lord and master,
He'll condescend to a new victim soon,
And make some patient waiter a sad loser.

VIII.

"Some patient waiter!" Such a one I know.
There was a time when I resolved, if ever
I could secure a modest competence,
I would be married; and the competence
Is now secure — but where is my resolve?
Shall I conclude 't is all fatality?
Leave it to chance, and take no active step
Myself to seek what I so hope to find?
Accepting it as heaven's fixed ordinance,

That man should change his single lot at will,
But woman be the sport of circumstance,
A purposeless and passive accident,
Inert as oysters waiting for a tide,
But not like oysters, sure of what they wait for?
"Ah! woman's strength is in passivity,"
Fastidio says, shaking his wise, wise head,
And withering me with a disdainful stare.
Nay! woman's strength is in developing,
In virtuous ways, all that is best in her.
No superstitious waiting then be mine!
No fancy that in coy, alluring arts,
Rather than action, modest and sincere,
Woman most worthily performs her part.
Here am I twenty-five, and all alone
In the wide world; yet having won the right,
By my own effort, to hew out my lot,
And create ties to cheer this arid waste.
How bleak and void my Future, if I stand
Waiting beside the stream, until some Prince —

Son of Queen Moonbeam by King Will-o'-the
   wisp —
Appears, and jumping from his gilded boat,
Lays heart and fortune at my idle feet!
Ye languid day-dreams, vanish! let me act!

But ah! Fastidio says, "A woman's wooing
Must always be offensive to a man
Of any dignity." The dignity
That modest truth can shock is far too frail
And sensitive to mate with love of mine,
Whose earnestness might crush the feeble hand
Linked in its own. So good by, dignity!
I shall survive the chill of your repulse.
Defiance, not of Nature's law, but Custom's,
Is what disturbs Fastidio. Does he think
That a *man's* wooing never is offensive
To *woman's* dignity? In either sex
The disaffection is not prompted by
The wooing but the wooer; love can never

Be an unwelcome tribute to the lover;
Though freedom premature, or forwardness
Unwarranted, may rightly fail to win.
And so I'll run my risk; for I confess —
(Keep the unuttered secret, sacred leaf!) —
That there is one whom I could love — could die
    for,
Would he but — Tears? Well, tears may come
    from strength
As well as weakness: I'll not grudge him these;
I'll not despair while I can shed a tear.

IX.

I've found him — seen him! The Directory
Gave me his residence. He keeps a school,
One for young ladies only; and at once
My coward heart hit on a good excuse
For calling on him: Would he take a pupil?
Rachel, my protégée? Of course he would.
A flush of tender, joyful wonderment,

Methought, illumed his face at seeing me;
Then, as it faded, I was grieved to mark
How pale and thin and worn with care he
 looked.
I took my leave, promising to return
Within a week; and on the outer steps
I met his father. "Turn and walk with me
A square or two," said I; and he complied.
"What ails him?" I inquired. "Only hard
 work:
He puts too much of conscience into it.
Needs help, but shrinks from debt, and so keeps
 on
Doing the labor two or three should share.
What shall I do, Miss Percival, to stop it?"
"I know not, — only something must be done,
And that at once," said I, in tones which made
The old man turn to get a look at me.
I hailed an omnibus, and there we parted. . . . .
What if I write Charles Lothian a letter?

Nay, I'll not skulk behind a sheet of paper,
But face to face say what I have to say.
This very evening must I call again.
Let a firm will bear up my fainting heart!

x.

And so at eight o'clock the carriage came,
And entering it I drove to Lothian's.
At last I was alone with him once more!
He had been sitting at a table heaped
With manuscripts, and these he was correcting.
"I'm here to interrupt all this," said I;
"Too long you've kept your brain upon the
    stretch:
Why be so heedless of your health, your life?"
"But what are they to you, Miss Percival?"
"And that is what I've come to let you know,"
Said I, emboldened by the offered foothold.
He flushed a little, only just a little, —
Replying, "*That* I'm curious to learn."

From Linda's Diary.

And then, like one who, in the dark, at first
Moves cautiously, but soon runs boldly on,
I said: "Rash gambler that I am, I've come
To put upon the hazard of a die
Much of my present and my future peace;
Perhaps to shock, repel, and anger you,
Since 't will not be unwarned that I offend.
I know you guess my purpose, and you shrink
From hearing me avow it; but I will,
And that in homely English unadorned.
I'm here to offer you my hand; the heart
That should go with it has preceded it,
And dwells with you, so you can claim your own,
Or gently bid it go, to trouble you
Never again. If 't is unwomanly
This to avow, then I'm unlike my sex,
Not false to my own nature,—ah! not false.
I must be true or die; I cannot play
A masker's part, disguising hopes that cling
Nearest my brooding heart. But, say the word,

'I cannot love you,' and the bird who leaves
The cage where he has pined will sooner try
To enter it again, than I return
To utter plaint of mine within your hearing"

With throbbing heart and burning face I ceased.
Twice, thrice he tried to stop me; but my words
Came all too quick and earnestly for that.
And then resigned he listened. I had seen,
Or dreamed I had, at first a sacred joy
At my avowal sparkle in his eyes,
And then an utter sadness follow it,
Which chilled me, and I knew that I had failed.

"O divine Pity! what will you not brave?"
He answered, and the dew was in his eyes, —
"You bring her here, even to abase herself
To rescue me! Too costly sacrifice!
Here do not dwell the Graces and the Loves,
But Drudgery is master of the house.

Dear lady, elsewhere seek the answering bloom."
A hope flashed up. "Do you suppose," said I,
"That any impulse less supreme than love —
Love bold to venture, but intemerate —
Could bring me here — that Pity could do this?"

"I believe all," he answered, "all you say;
But do not bid me whisper more than this:
The circumstances that environ me,
And which none know, — not even my father knows, —
Shut me out utterly from any hope
Of marriage or of love. A wretch in prison
Might better dream of marrying than I.
But O sweet lady! rashly generous, —
Around whom, a protecting atmosphere,
Floats Purity, and sends her messengers
With flaming swords to guard each avenue
From thoughts unholy and approaches base, —
Thou who hast made an act I deemed uncomely

Seem beautiful and gracious, — do not doubt
My memory of thy worth shall be the same,
Only expanded, lifted up, and touched
With light as dear as sunset radiance
To summer trees after a thunder-storm."

And there was silence then between us two.
Thought of myself was lost in thought for him.
What was my wreck of joy, compared with his?
Health, youth, and competence were mine, and
    he
Was staking all of his to save another.
If my winged hopes fell fluttering to the ground,
Regrets and disappointments were forgotten
In the reflection, He, then, is unhappy!
"Good by!" at length I said, giving my hand:
"Even as I was believed, will I believe.
You do not deal in hollow compliment;
And we shall meet again if you 're content.
The good time will return — and I 'll return!"

"If you return, the good time will return
And stay as long as you remain," said he.

XI.

It is as I supposed: an obstacle
Which his assumption of his father's debts
Has raised before him unexpectedly!
I did not let a day go by before
I saw the elder Lothian, and he,
Distressed by what I told him of a secret,
Applied himself to hunting up a key
To the mysterious grief: at last he got it,
Though not by means that I could justify.
In Charles's private escritoire he found
A memorandum that explained it all.
Among the obligations overlooked,
In settling up the firm's accounts, was one
Of fifty thousand dollars, payable
To an estate, the representatives
Of which were six small children and a widow,

Dependent now on what they could derive
Of income from this debt; and manfully
Charles shoulders it, although it crushes him;
And hopes to keep his father ignorant.
I can command one quarter of the sum
Already — but the rest? That staggers me.
And yet why should I falter? Look at *him!*
Let his example be my high incentive.
I'll be his helpmate, and he shall not know it.
Poor Charles! I'll toil for him, — to him devote
All that I have of energy and skill,
All I acquire. Ambition shall not mount
Less loftily for having Love to help it.
Come forth, my easel! All thy work has been
Girl's play till now; now will I truly venture.
I've a new object now — to rescue *him!*
And he shall never know his rescuer
From lips of mine, — no, though I die for it,
With the sweet secret undisclosed, — my heart
Glad in the love he never may requite!

VIII.

FROM MEREDITH'S DIARY.

I.

INCALCULABLY selfish and corrupt,
  Well may man need a sacrifice divine
To expiate infinity of sin.
Few but a priest can know the fearful depth
Of human wickedness. At times I shrink
Faint and amazed at what I have to learn:
And then I wonder that the Saviour said
His yoke is easy and his burden light.
Ah! how these very murmurs at my lot

Show that not yet into my heart has crept
That peace of God which passeth understanding!

II.

Among my hearers lately there has been
A lady all attention to my words:
Thrice have I seen that she was deeply moved;
And to confession yesterday she came.
Let me here call her Harriet. She is
By education Protestant, but wavers,
Feeling the ground beneath her insecure,
And would be led unto the rock that is
Higher than she. A valuable convert;
Not young; in feeble health; taxed for two
    millions;
And she would found, out of her ample means,
A home for orphans and neglected children.
Heaven give me power to lead the stray one safe
Into the only fold; securing thus
Aid for the church, salvation for herself!

III.

A summons took me to her house to-day.
Her mother and her step-father compose
With Harriet the household. I refrain
From putting real names on paper here.
Let me then call the man's name, Denison;
He's somewhat younger than his wife, a lady
Advanced in years, but her heart wholly set
On the frivolities of fashion still.
I see the situation at a glance:
A mercenary marriage on the part
Of Denison, whose hungry eyes are fixed
Upon the daughter's property; the mother
Under his evil influence, and expecting
The daughter to die soon, without a will,
Thus leaving all to them; — and Harriet
Not quite so dull but she can penetrate
Denison's motive and her mother's hope!
A sad state for an invalid who feels
That any hour may be her last! To-day

Harriet confessed; for she has been alarmed
By some bad symptoms lately. As she urged it,
I sent word to the bishop, and he came,
And she was formally confirmed, and taken
Unto the bosom of the Church, and there
May her poor toiling spirit find repose!

IV.

Another summons! In the drawing-room,
Whom should I meet but Denison? His stare
Had something vicious in it; but we bowed,
And he remarked: "I hear that Harriet,
Caught in your Catholic net, is turning saint.
No foul play, priest! She's not in a condition
To make a will, or give away her money.
Remember that, and do not waste your words."
My color rose, and the brute Adam in me
Would, uncontrolled, have surely knocked him
    down.
But I cast off temptation, and replied:

"Sir, I'm responsible to God, not man."
I left him, and passed on to Harriet.
I found her greatly moved; an interview
She had been having with her mother caused
The agitation. "Take me hence!" she cried;
"I'll not remain another day or hour
Under this roof. I tell you, I'm not safe
With these two, watching, dogging, maddening
 me."
She rang the bell, and to the servant said:
"My carriage, and that quickly!" Then to me:
"I'll show them that I'm mistress of my fortune
And of myself. Call on me in an hour
At the Fifth Avenue Hotel, for there
Henceforth I make my home." And there
I called, as she had ordered, and we met
In her own parlor. "What I wish," said she,
"Is to give all I have, without reserve,
For the foundation that I've planned. I'll
 send

Directions to my lawyer, and the papers
Shall be prepared at once." — " Before you do it,
Let me learn more of you and yours," said I :
" Who was your father ? " Then, to my surprise,
I learnt that he was one whom I had met
Some years before, — in his death-hour had met.
" But you 've a sister ? " suddenly I asked.
Surprised, she answered : " A half-sister — yes —
I 've seen her only once ; for many years
I lived in Europe ; she 's in England now,
And married happily. On three occasions
I 've sent her money." — " Do you correspond ? "
" Not often ; here are letters from her, full
Of thanks for all I 've given her." — " In your will
Shall you remember her ? " — " If you advise it.".
" Then I advise a liberal bequest.
And now I must attend a sufferer
Who waits my help." — " Father, I would confess."

"Daughter, be quick: I listen." Harriet
Then gave a sad recital of a trial
And a divorce; and (but reluctantly)
Told of a terrible suspicion, born
Of a remark, dropped by a servant once,
Concerning her unlikeness to her father:
But never could she wring a confirmation
Of the distressing story from her mother.
"Tell her," said I, "you mean to leave your sister
A handsome legacy." She promised this.
Then saying I would call the following day,
I hurried off to see poor Ellen Blount.

V.

A new surprise! There, by the patient's bed,
I came on Linda, Harriet's half-sister!
(Reputed so, at least, but here's a doubt.)
I questioned her, and now am satisfied
Treason and forgery have been at work,
Defeating Harriet's sisterly intent;

Moreover, that the harrowing surmise,
Waked by a servant's gossip overheard,
Is, in all probability, the truth!
And, if we so accept it, what can I
Advise but Harriet's complete surrender
Of all her fortune to the real child
And proper heir of Albert Percival?
But ah! 't is now devoted to the Church!
Here 's a divided duty; I must lay
The case before a higher power than mine.

VI.

I 've had a long discussion with the bishop.
I placed before him all the facts, beginning
With those of my own presence at the death
Of Linda's parents; of her father's letter
Received that day, communicating news
Of Kenrick's large bequest; the father's effort
In dying to convey in legal form
To his child Linda all this property;

The failure of the effort; his decease,
And all I knew of subsequent events.
And the good bishop, after careful thought,
Replied: "Some way the mother must be brought
To full confession. Of her guilt no doubt!"
I told him I had charged it on the daughter
To tell her mother of the legacy
Designed for Linda; this, perchance, might wring
Confession from the guilty one. He seemed
To think it not unlikely, and remarked:
"When that is got, there's but a single course
For you to urge on Harriet; for, my son,
I need not tell a Christian gentleman,
Not to say priest, that this peculiar case
We must decide precisely as we would
If the Church had in it no interest:
Let Harriet at once give up, convey,
Not bequeath merely, all she has to Linda.
Till she does this, her soul will be in peril;
When she does this, she shall be made the ward

Of Holy Church, and cared for to the end."
I kissed his hand and left. How his high thoughts
Poured round my path a flood of light divine!
Why did I hesitate, since he could make
The path of duty so directly clear!

VII.

Harriet's intimation to her mother
That she should leave a good part of her wealth
To her half-sister brought things to a crisis.
To-day my visit found the two together:
Harriet, in an agony of tears,
Cried to me, as I entered, — " 'T is all true!
God! She confesses it — confesses it!
Confesses, too, she never sent the money,
And that the letters were all forgeries!
And thinks, by this confession, to secure
My fortune to herself! Ah! Can this woman
Be, then, my mother?"
      Hereupon the woman,

Crimson with rage at being thus exposed,
Exclaimed, "Unnatural daughter —" But before
Her wrath could vent itself, she, with a groan,
Fell in convulsions. Medical assistance
Was had at once. Then Denison came in,
Aghast at what had happened; for he knew
His wife's estate was all in lands and houses,
And would, if she should die, be Harriet's,
Since the old lady superstitiously
Had still put off the making of a will.
All help was vain, and drugs were powerless.
Paralysis had struck the heated brain,
Driving from mortal hold the consciousness:
It reappeared not in one outward sign,
And before midnight life had left the clay.

VIII.

Meek and submissive as a little child
Is Harriet now; she has no will but that

The Church imposes as the will divine.
"Your fortune, nearly doubled by this death,
Must all," said I, " be now conveyed to Linda."
"Let it be done," she cried, " before I sleep!"
And it was done to-night — securely done, —
I being Linda's representative.
To-morrow I must take her the good news.

IX.

After the storm, the rainbow, child of light!
Such the transition, as I pass to Linda!
I found her hard at work upon a picture.
With wonder at Heaven's ways she heard my
    news.
Shocked at the tragic death, she did not hide
Her satisfaction at the tardy act
Bringing the restitution of her own.
Three things she asked; one was that I would
    place
At once a certain person in possession

Of a large sum, not letting him find out
From whom it came; another was to have
This great change in her fortunes kept a secret
As long as she might wish; the third and last
Was that she might be privileged to wait
On Harriet with a sister's loving care.
All which I promised readily should be,
So far as my poor human will could order.
Said Linda then: "Tell Harriet, her scheme
For others' welfare shall not wholly fail;
That in your hands I'll place a sum sufficient
To plant the *germ* at least of what she planned."

x.

I've taken my last look of Harriet:
She died in Linda's arms, and comforted
With all the Church could give of heavenly hope.
Slowly and imperceptibly does Time
Work out the dreadful problem of our sins!
Not often do we see it solved as here

In plain results which he who runs may read.
Not always is the sinner's punishment
Shown in this world. May the Eternal Mercy
Cleanse us from secret faults, nor, while we mark
Another's foulness, blind us to our own!

IX.

BESIDE THE LAKE.

THE sun of August from a clear blue sky
    Shone on Lake Saranac. The South-wind
        stirred
Mildly the woods encircling, that threw down
A purple shadow on the liquid smoothness
Glassing the eastern border, while the west
Lay bared to light.
                Wild, virgin nature all!
Except that here and there a partial clearing,

Made by the sportsman's axe for summer tents,
Dented the massive verdure, and revealed
A little slope of bank, dotted with stumps
And brown with slender aromatic leaves
Shed from the pine, the hemlock, and the fir
In layers that gave a soft and slippery carpet.

Near one of these small openings where the breeze
Crept resinous and cool from evergreens
Behind them, while the sun blazed bright before, —
Where with the pine-trees' vapory depth of hue
The whiteness of a spacious tent contrasted,
Beside which, on a staff, the nation's flag
Flung out its crimson with protecting pride, —
Reclined a wife and husband, looking down
Less on the glorious lake than on the glory
That, through a gauzy veil, played round the head

Of a reposing infant, golden-tressed,
Asleep upon a deer-skin at their feet,
While a huge dog kept watchful guard beyond:
For there lay little Mary Merivale.

Boats on the lake showed that this group de-
    tached
Were part of a well-chosen company.
Here children ran and frolicked on the beach;
There an old man, rowed by two guides, stood
    up
With rod and line and reel, while swiftly flew
The reel, announcing that a vigorous trout
Just then had seized the hook. Came the loud
    cry, —
"Look, Charles! Look, Linda! See me land
    him now!
Don't touch him with your scoop, men! I can
    fetch him," —
In tones not unfamiliar to our ears.

And there, six boats swept by, from which the voices
Of merry children and their elder friends —
Mothers and fathers, teachers, faded aunts,
Dyspeptic uncles, wonderfully cured
All by this tonic, Adirondack air —
Came musical and loud : a strange collection,
Winnowed by Rachel (now the important queen
Of all this sanitary revelry)
From her acquaintance in the public schools;
Whence her quick sympathies had carried her
Straight to the overworked, the poor, the ailing,
Among the families of her associates,
When Linda planned this happy enterprise
Of a grand camping-out for one whole month.
The blind aunt and the grandmother, of course,
High and important persons, Rachel's aids,
Graced the occasion ; for the ancient dame
Had lived in such a region in her youth,
And in all sylvan craft was proudly wise :

Declaring that this taste of life would add
Some ten years to her eighty-five, at least.

On went the boats, all large and safely manned,
In competition not too venturesome.
Then, from a rocky outlook on the hill,
There came a gush of music from a band,
Employed to cheer with timely melody
This strange encampment in the wilderness.
Hark! Every voice is hushed as down the lake
The breathing clarions accordant send
The tune of "Love Not" to each eager ear!
The very infant, in its slumber, smiled
As if a dream of some old paradise
Had been awakened by the ravishment.

"Look at the child!" cried Linda; "mark that
    smile!
All heaven reflected in a dew-drop! See!"
"And all the world grasped in that little fist, —

At least as we esteem the world!" cried Charles.
"And yet," said Linda, "'t is a glorious world :
See how those families enjoy themselves!"
" And who created all this happiness?"
The husband said,—"who, after God, but Linda?
Who spends her money, not in rearing piles
Of cold and costly marble for her pride,—
Not in great banquets for the rich and gay
Who need them not, and laugh at those who
    give,—
Where, at one feast, enough is spent to make
All these poor people radiant for a month,—
But in exhilarations coming from
Communicated joy and health and life,—
The happiness that 's found in making happy."

"All selfishness!" cried Linda ; " selfishness!
I seek my happiness, and others theirs ;
Only my tastes are different ; more plebeian,
Haply, they 'd say ; but, husband mine, reflect!

You, too, I fear, are lacking in refinement:
Would this have been, had you not acquiesced
In all these vulgar freaks, and found content,
Like me, in giving pleasure to the needy?
And tell me — passing to another point —
Where would have been the monarch of this joy,
That little child, — that antepast of bliss
Such as the angels taste, — had I recoiled
From daring as I did, even when I knew
He I most wished to win would think me bold?"

"Ah! little wife," cried Charles, "I've half a mind
To tell you what I've never told you yet.
Yes, I *will* tell you all, although it may
End the complacent thought that Linda did it —
Did it by simply daring to propose!
Know, then, a constant track of you I kept,
Even while I seemed to shun you. I could kneel
Before your recollection in my heart,

When you regarded me as shy and cold.
And, while by poverty held reticent,
I saw, supreme among my hopes, but Linda!
Before we left the sea-side I had learnt,
Through gossip of my worthy landlady,
Where you would go, returning to New York.
I found your house; I passed it more than once
When, like a beacon, shone your study-lamp.
The very night before you called upon me
To ask, would I take Rachel as my pupil,
(How kind in you to patronize my school!)
I sought an anodyne for my despair
In watching for your shadow on the curtain.

"Discovery of that unexpected debt,
Owed by my father, killed the last faint hope
Which I had cherished; and our interview —
Your daring offer of this little hand —
But made me emulous to equal you
In self-renouncing generosity;

And so, I frankly told you what I told:
That love and marriage were not in my lot.

"Ten days elapsed, and then from utter gloom
I sprang to cheerful light. My father's partner,
The man named Judd, who robbed us all one day,
Had a compunctious interval, and sent
A hundred thousand dollars back to us —
Why do you smile?"

     "Go on. 'T is worth a smile."

"That very day I cleared myself from debt;
That very day I sued for Linda's hand;
That very day she gave it willingly;
And the next month beheld us two made one.
And so it would have been, if you, my dear,
Had made no sign, and waited patiently.
But ah! what luck was mine! After two days,
The news arrived that Linda was an heiress.
An heiress! Think of it; and I had said,

Never, no, never would I wed an heiress!
But 't was too late for scruples; I was married, —
Caught in the trap I always meant to shun!"

Then Linda, mischief in her smile, exclaimed:
"O simple Charles! The innocent dear man!
Who doubts but woman ought to hold her
    tongue,
And wait till he, the preordained, appear?
That hundred thousand dollars, you are sure,
Was from your father's partner — was from Judd?"

"Of course it was, — from Judd, and no one else!
Who could have sent the money, if not Judd?
No doubt it came from Judd! My father said,
'T was conscience-money, and restored by Judd,
Who had become a deacon in the Church.
Why did you ask me whether I was sure
The hundred thousand dollars came from Judd?
What are you smiling at, provoking Linda?"

"O, you 're so quick, so clever, all you men!
And women are so dull and credulous,
So easily duped, when left to go alone!
What you would prove is, that my daring step,
In being first to make a declaration,
Was needless, since priority in love
Was yours, and your intention would have brought
The same result about without my seeking.
Know then, the money was not yours until
I 'd got the news of my recovered fortune;
From me the money came, and only me;
And all that story of a Judd, turned deacon,
Grown penitent and making restitution,
Was a mere myth, invented by your father,
Lest you might hesitate to take the money.
Now if I had not sought you as I did,
And if I had not put you to the test,
And if I had not learnt your secret grief,
We might have lived till we were gray and bent
Before a step of yours had brought us nearer."

"Outflanked! I own it, and I give it up!"
Cried Charles, all flushing with astonishment:
"But how I'll rate that ancient fisherman,
My graceless father, for deceiving me!
See him stand there, as if with conscience void,
Throwing the line for innocent, fat trout!
With that grave face, saying the money came
From Judd, — from Deacon Judd! I'll deacon
    him!"

"What! you regret it, do you, Master Charles?
The crooked ways that brought you where you are
You would make straight, and have the past un-
    done?
To think that by a woman you've been wooed,
To think that by a woman you've been won,
Is thought too humbling and too scandalous;
Is an indignity too hard to bear!
Oh! well, sir, well; do as you please; the child
Goes with its mother, though; remember that."

And here the infant threw its eyelids back,
Revealing orbs, blue as the shadows cast
On Saranac's blue by overhanging woods.
Said Lothian, snatching up the smiling wonder,
And handing it, with kisses, to the mother:
"Take all your woman's rights; even this, the best:
Are we not each the richer by the sharing
Of such a gift? I'll not regret your daring."

NOTES.

PAGE 11.

"Oh! lacking love and best experience."

An extreme Materialism here comes to the support of a grim theology. In his "Physiology and Pathology of the Mind," Dr. Maudsley says: "To talk about the purity and innocence of a child's mind is a part of that poetical idealism and willing hypocrisy by which man ignores realities and delights to walk in a vain show." Such sweeping generalizations do not inspire confidence in the writer's prudence. Christ was nearer the truth when he said, concerning little children, — "Of such is the kingdom of heaven."

PAGE 64.

" Few honorable outlooks for support,
Excepting marriage."

Referring to the fact that in Massachusetts, during the ten years from 1859 to 1869, the increase of crime among women has been much greater than among men, Miss Catherine Beecher remarks : " But turning from these (the criminal class) to the daughters of the most wealthy class, those who have generous and devoted aspirations also feel that for them, too, there is no opening, no promotion, no career, except that of marriage, — *and for this they are trained to feel that it is disgraceful to seek. They have nothing to do but wait to be sought. Trained to believe marriage their highest boon, they are disgraced for seeking it, and must affect indifference.*

"Meantime to do anything to earn their own independence is what father and brothers would deem a disgrace to themselves and their family. For women of high position to work for their livelihood, in most cases custom decrees as disgraceful. And then, if cast down by poverty, they have been trained to nothing that would earn a support, or, if by chance they have some resource, all avenues for its employment are thronged with needy applicants."

This is but a very mild statement of the social fictions under which woman is now suffering in mind, body, and estate; but it is valuable as coming from a witness who hopes that some less radical remedy than female suffrage will be found for existing evils. If the remedy lies with woman herself, as all admit, how can we expect her to act efficiently until she is a modifying force in legislation?

PAGE 65.

" *Unions, no priest, no church can sanctify.*"

" The most absurd notions," says J. A. St. John, " have prevailed on the subject of matrimony. Marriage, it is said, is a divine institution, therefore marriages are made in heaven; but the consequence does not at all follow; the meaning of the former proposition simply being that God originally ordained that men and women should be united in wedlock; but that he determined what particular men and women should be united, every day's experience proves to be false. It is admitted on all hands that marriage is intended to confer happiness on those who wed. Now, if it be found that marriage does not confer happiness on them, it is an undoubted proof that they ought not to have been united, and that the sooner they separate the better; but from accepting this doctrine some persons are deterred by misrepresentations of scripture, others by views of policy, and others again by an entire indifference to human happiness. They regard men and women as mere animals, and, provided they have children, and rear them, nothing more."

"It is incredible," says Milton, " how cold, how dull, and far from all fellow-feeling we are, *without the spur of self-concernment!*"

Page 72.

"Behold the world's ideal of a wife!"

"All women," says John Stuart Mill, "are brought up from their very earliest years in the belief that their ideal character is the very opposite to that of man; not self-will and self-government by self-control, but submission and yielding to the control of others. . . . . What is now called the nature of women is an eminently artificial thing, — the result of forced repression in some directions, unnatural stimulation in others."

The cowardice that is looked upon as disgraceful in a man is regarded by many as rather honorable than otherwise in a woman. False notions, inherited from chivalrous times, and growing out of the state of subjection in which woman has been bred, have generated this inconsistency. The truth is that courage is honorable to both sexes; to a Grace Darling and an Ida Lewis, a Madame Roland and a Florence Nightingale, as well as to a Bayard and a Shaw, a Napoleon and a Farragut.

Page 73.

"That moment should the intimate relations
Of marriage end, and a release be found!"

In the United States the action of certain State legislatures, in increasing the facilities for divorce, has been a subject of alarm among persons bred under the influences of a more conservative system. It would be difficult to show as yet whether social morality is harmed or helped by the increased freedom. Nothing can be more deceptive and unsatisfactory than the statistics offered on both sides of the question. It is generally admitted, we believe, that in those countries where divorce is most difficult, the number of illegitimate births is largest, and the reputation of married women is most questionable. In the nature of things, much of the prevalent immorality being furtive and clandestine, it is impossible to estimate the extent of the evils growing out of illiberal laws in relation to matrimony. In any legislation on the subject women should have a voice.

PAGE 80.

"*Unlike the Church, I look on marriage as
A civil contract, not a sacrament.*"

Kenrick here refers of course to the Catholic Church, whose theory of marriage, namely, that it is a sacrament and indissoluble, when once contracted according to the forms of the Church, still influences the legislation and social prejudices of Protestant communities in respect to their own religious forms of marriage. It was not till the twelfth century, and under the auspices of Pope Innocent III., that divorce was prohibited by the civil as well as the canon law. But it is only a marriage between Catholics that is indissoluble under the Catholic system. In the case of a marriage of Protestants, the tie is not regarded as binding. A dissolution was actually granted in such a case where one of the parties turned Catholic, in 1857, by the bishop of Rio Janeiro, who pronounced an uncanonical marriage null and void. Modern legislation in establishing the validity of civil marriages aimed a severe blow at ecclesiastical privilege.

To Rome and not to the Bible we must go for all the authority we can produce for denying that marriage is simply a civil contract. The form, binding one man to one woman, had its origin outside of the Bible. Up to the time of Charlemagne in the eighth century, polygamy and concubinage were common among Christians and countenanced by the Church. Even Luther seems to have had somewhat lax, though not unscriptural, notions on the subject. When Philip, landgrave of Hesse-Cassel, wanted to take another wife, and threatened to get a dispensation from the Pope for the purpose, Luther convoked a synod, composed of six of his proselytes, who declared that marriage is merely a civil contract; that they could find no passage in the Holy Scriptures ordaining monogamy; and they consequently signed a decree permitting Philip to take a second wife without repudiating his first.

In that reconstruction of laws, threatened by the movement in behalf of female suffrage, it is not probable that the patriarchal institution of polygamy will be regarded otherwise than as debasing to both sexes; but perhaps a greater latitude of divorce will be sought as not inconsistent with public morality. Looking at the question abstractly, and apart from all religious and social prejudice, it certainly seems the height of cruelty and absurdity to compel parties to keep up the relations of man and wife when one of them feels towards the other either a physical repugnance or a moral dislike. The impediments often raised by our courts in the way of divorce are gross relics of barbarism, and will be abolished by a higher legislative morality.

"Whoso," says Milton, "prefers either matrimony or other ordinance before the good of man and the plain exigence of charity, let him profess Papist or Protestant or what he will, he is no better than a pharisee, and understands not the gospel; whom, as a misinterpreter of Christ, I openly protest against." And, in another passage, he rebukes those who would rest " in the mere element of the text," as favoring " the policy of the Devil to make that gracious ordinance (of marriage) become insupportable, that what with men not daring to venture upon wedlock, and what with men wearied out of it, all inordinate license might abound."

Mr. J. A. St. John, editor of the Prose Works of Milton, remarks in reference to the marriage law as it now stands in England: —

"*Having been invented and established by men, it is calculated to bear with extreme severity on women*, who are daily subjected to wrongs and hardships which they would not endure, were the relief of divorce open to them. Those who take a different view descant upon the encouragement which would, they say, be given to immorality were divorce made easy. But the contrary is the truth.

"It is in behalf of morals, and for the sake of imparting a higher tone to the feelings of society, that the present unnatural system should be abolished. Where, what Milton calls, an unconjugal mind exists, there must be unconjugal manners; and to what these lead no one need be told. Where marriage is indissoluble, people presume upon that fact to transgress its laws, which they would not do were it legally practicable to obtain immediate redress.

"However, there is a great indisposition in mankind to innovate in legislation; and they had generally rather be miserable according to rule than free and happy on a novel principle. . . . . Whenever it clearly appears that man and wife can no longer live together in peace and harmony, their separation would be far more beneficial to themselves and favorable to morals, than their compulsory union. Milton's notions of married life are highly flattering to women, whom he evidently contemplates as the equal companions of men."

Page 156.
" Give her the suffrage."

In one of his pamphlets in behalf of women's suffrage, Professor F. W. Newman of England, a man of widest culture and noblest sympathies, and always among the ablest and foremost in good works, remarks: "It is useless to reply that women have not political knowledge. Hitherto they have had little motive to acquire it. But how much of such knowledge have those male voters had, whom, for two hundred years past, candidates for the place of M. P. have made drunk in the tippling-houses? The arguments used against female suffrage simply show that there is nothing valid to be said. Women have, *prima facie*, the same right as men."

Page 160.
" Not by evading or profaning Nature."

In his recent "History of European Morals," Mr. Lecky, referring to the fact that the prevalent doctrine is, that the very highest interest of society is not to stimulate but to restrain multiplication, diminishing the number of marriages and of children, presents the following comments: —

"In consequence of this belief, and of the many factitious wants that accompany a luxurious civilization, a very large and increasing proportion of women are left to make their way in life without any male protector, and the difficulties they have to encounter through physical weakness have been most unnaturally and most fearfully aggravated by laws and customs which, resting on the old assumption that every woman should be a wife, habitually deprive them of the pecuniary and educational advantages of men, exclude them absolutely from very many of the employments in which they might earn a subsistence, encumber their course in others by a heartless ridicule or by a steady disapprobation, and consign, in consequence, many thousands to the most extreme and agonizing poverty, and perhaps a still larger number to the paths of vice.

"At the same time a momentous revolution, the effects of which can as yet be but imperfectly descried, has taken place in the chief spheres of female industry that remain. The progress of machinery has destroyed its domestic character. The distaff has fallen from the hand. The needle is being rapidly superseded, and the work which, from the days of Homer to the present century, was accomplished in the centre of the family, has been transferred to the crowded manufactory."

The necessity of those reforms which many noble women are now urging upon public attention is clearly set forth in eloquent facts like these.

PAGE 198.

"*Is against nature.*"

A curious instance of the temerity with which flagrant errors are pressed into the service of criticism is presented in some remarks in the *N. Y. Nation*. "There is probably," it says, "no incident of woman's condition which is more clearly natural than her passivity in all that relates to marriage. In waiting to be wooed, she not only complies with one of the conventional proprieties, but obeys what appears to be a law of sex, *not amongst human beings only, but among all animals.*"

These remarks have been adopted by many American journalists, and have been accepted perhaps by many readers as settling the whole question with scientific accuracy and force, so far as analogies drawn from the habits of the lower animals can settle it. But if the critic, while buttering his daily bread or putting cream into his daily coffee, had acquainted himself with the habits of the useful animal to which he is indebted, he would never have been guilty of so prodigious a blunder. So far from passively "waiting to be wooed," the cow, when the sexual impulse is awakened, will disturb the whole neighborhood by her bellowings. Should the critic reply that this is because she is kept in an unnatural state of restraint, such reply would add only additional force to the contradiction of the argument which he would offer.

Other examples in abundance, in confutation of his assumption, could no doubt be furnished. But even were that assumption true, we might sometimes be led to rather awkward results if we were to take the habits of the lower animals as authoritative. Certain animals have not infrequently an eccentric habit of destroying their offspring. Some of our Chinese brethren, borrowing a hint perhaps from the brute creation, are said to think it no sin to kill such female children as they have no use for. We hope that no enterprising critic will recommend such a solution as this of the woman problem.

THE END.

Cambridge: Electrotyped and Printed by Welch, Bigelow, & Co.

www.ingramcontent.com/pod-product-compliance
Lightning Source LLC
Chambersburg PA
CBHW031251250426
43672CB00029BA/2002